TWAYNE'S WORLD AUTHORS SERIES
A Survey of the World's Literature

Sylvia E. Bowman, Indiana University
GENERAL EDITOR

FRANCE

Maxwell A. Smith, Guerry Professor of French, Emeritus
The University of Chattanooga
Former Visiting Professor in Modern Languages
The Florida State University
EDITOR

Jean Mairet

TWAS 358

Photo courtesy of Bibliothèque Nationale, Paris

Jean Mairet

By WILLIAM A. BUNCH
Kansas State University

TWAYNE PUBLISHERS
A DIVISION OF G. K. HALL & CO., BOSTON

842.4
M228X
B942

Copyright © 1975 by G. K. Hall & Co.

All Rights Reserved

Library of Congress Cataloging in Publication Data

Bunch, William A.
 Jean Mairet.

163 p. / poet / 21

 (Twayne's world authors series; TWAS 358: France)
 Bibliography: pp. 157–60.
 Includes index.
 1. Mairet, Jean de, 1604–1686.
PQ1818.M6Z6   842'.4   74-34122
ISBN 0-8057-2565-2

MANUFACTURED IN THE UNITED STATES OF AMERICA

Contents

About the Author
Preface
Chronology
1. Mairet's Life   11
2. First Attempts and First Success   28
3. Mairet and Progress of the Unities   57
4. Comic Interlude: *Les Galanteries du duc d'Ossonne*   84
5. The Tragedies   97
6. The Final Tragicomedies   132
   Conclusion   149
   Notes and References   151
   Selected Bibliography   157
   Index   161

About the Author

William A. Bunch received his B.A. *cum laude* in French from Hanover College, Hanover, Indiana in 1965. He continued his studies at the University of Wisconsin (M.A., 1966) and at the University of Texas where he was conferred the doctoral degree in French in 1972. He has taught at the University of Wisconsin—Green Bay, the University of Texas—Austin, and the Lycée Henri IV in Paris. Presently he holds the position Assistant Professor in the Department of Modern Languages, Kansas State University. His research interests include French drama through the gamut of its existence, in particular the early seventeenth century and the twentieth century, and the literature of the Baroque.

Preface

After the presentation of his tragedy *Sophonisbe* in 1634 the critics and the public alike acclaimed Jean Mairet the leading dramatist of his generation. The path of his career, each success building and solidifying his talent, seemed to project him toward that lasting reputation reserved only for the greatest authors. And yet scarcely three years later he found himself attacked, on the defensive, and involved in a petty personal quarrel which in many respects signaled the end of his short-lived glory. Mairet's conduct during the famous *Querelle du Cid*, deportment often unbecoming a man of his stature, underlined the great frustration he felt at seeing himself quite literally dethroned by an upstart from the provinces, Pierre Corneille. The quarrel struck Mairet as he had begun his decline. After that affair he was not only eclipsed by Corneille but betrayed by his own weakening talents, until in 1640 he retired from the literary world. The promise of the early 1630s had borne no fruit for the author. He had not achieved the desired enduring success. Although he lived until 1686, he never again set pen to paper to compose a dramatic poem. His career had lasted from 1625 to 1640, a span of fifteen years during which time he composed twelve plays. Among them were three or four of the most successful and most influential dramatic works written in the first third of the seventeenth century.

Ever since his quarrel with Corneille, although not because of it, Mairet has remained a secondary figure in the history of seventeenth-century French dramatic literature. Scholars accord him a footnote, a paragraph, a chapter at best in which prime interest centers on his *Sophonisbe* as the first French tragedy to respect the three unities. His career becomes one moment, often dismissed as an aberrant one for lack of context.

Almost one hundred years have passed since a book-length study has appeared on the works of Jean Mairet. One may ask, not without reason, if it would not serve literature and literary history more if he were to remain as he is, a relatively forgotten figure who wrote one important tragedy. Does Mairet need or even merit resurrecting? Without tossing hyperboles of praise to the winds, let it be understood that the present study does not intend to carve a new niche in literary history for the author, proclaim his superiority to his old rival Corneille, or even criticize as totally unjustified the neglect into which he has fallen. Before Corneille, Mairet was the most important French dramatic author of his time, as before Mairet it was Alexandre Hardy. The author's position proves to be special, resting as it does on the very threshold of the mature period of seventeenth-century French drama. Writing in a transitional era, Mairet deserves attention both insofar as he is representative of that age and as he differs from it. The author's particular strengths lie in both areas, his use of the common themes and his inventions. Through an examination of his twelve dramatic poems and the literary context surrounding them this study hopes to bring Mairet's talent as well as his role in the development of French drama to light. Since Mairet is in large part representative of his age, a study of the author also provides greater understanding of the complex currents present in the formative years of French classical drama, the late 1620s and the 1630s. A brief biography of the author is included to aid in comprehending both the man and his time. It rests largely on Mairet's own account of his life through letters written during the *Querelle* and the dedications of his plays, with additional information from other contemporary sources. Translations from the letters and from Mairet's works are all my own.

I would like to take this opportunity to express my gratitude to Dr. Gary B. Rodgers of Harvard University for his time and numerous suggestions during the preparation of the manuscript, and to Dr. A. Donald Sellstrom of the University of Texas for his direction in the initial stages of this work.

WILLIAM A. BUNCH

Kansas State University

Chronology

1604   May 10, baptism of Jean Mairet, in Besançon, parish of St. Pierre. His birth probably took place a few days previous to that date, since the family members were devout Catholics.

1625   Date of Mairet's entrance into the service of Henri II, duc de Montmorency.

1625   *Chryséide et Arimand*, tragi-comédie pastorale, presented at the Hôtel de Bourgogne. Mairet's first play, published without his knowledge in 1630.

1626   *Sylvie*, tragi-comédie pastorale, also presented at the Hôtel de Bourgogne. Mairet's first great success. Published 1632.

late 1629– early 1630   *Silvanire*, tragi-comédie régulière. Presented at the Hôtel de Bourgogne and published in 1631.

1632   October 30, execution of the duc de Montmorency. Mairet passed into the service of the comte de Belin shortly thereafter.

1632–1633   *Les Galanteries du duc d'Ossonne*, comédie. Staged by the troupe of the Théâtre du Marais, published 1636.

1633   *Virginie*, tragi-comédie. Théâtre du Marais, published 1635.

1634   *Sophonisbe*, tragédie. Presented with great success at the Théâtre du Marais, published 1635.

1635   *Marc Antoine ou la Cléopâtre*, tragédie. Théâtre du Marais, published 1637.

late 1637   *Le Grand et dernier Solyman ou la Mort de Mustapha*, tragédie. Presented at the Hôtel de Bourgogne, published 1639.

1637   February–October, the quarrel of the *Cid*.

late 1637	*L'Illustre Corsaire*, tragi-comédie. Hôtel de Bourgogne, published 1640.
early 1638	*Roland furieux*, tragi-comédie. Hôtel de Bourgogne, published 1640.
late 1638– early 1639	*Athénaïs*, tragi-comédie. Hôtel de Bourgogne, published 1642.
1640	*Sidonie*, tragi-comédie héroïque. Staged by the company of the Hôtel de Bourgogne, published 1643. Mairet abandoned the theater after the failure of this play.
1647	July 3, marriage contract signed between Jean Mairet and Jeanne de Cardouan.
1648	Mairet became the diplomatic agent in Paris for his native province, Franche-Comté.
1649– 1651	He negotiated two treaties of neutrality for the province.
1653	Mazarin banished Mairet from the court and from Paris. He returned to Besançon.
1668	Mairet received his letters of nobility from the Emperor Leopold entitling him and his brother's children to use the particle "de."
1686	January 31, death of Jean de Mairet in Besançon.

CHAPTER 1

Mairet's Life

I Early Life

WHEN the quarrel of the *Cid* broke out in early 1637 between Corneille and the other authors, Jean Mairet was an established writer with several successful plays to his credit. He justifiably believed himself the leading dramatist of his generation and dramatic poetry's reigning favorite. In part because of the sudden eclipse that fell on him with Corneille's triumph, his blatant self-adulation, which triggered the quarrel, angered Mairet. In his response to Corneille's *Excuse à Ariste* he chastised the younger man as an upstart claiming credit that should rightly have fallen to Guillén de Castro, from whom he stole the play.[1] In his reply, a pamphlet entitled *Advertissement au Besançonnois Mairet*, Corneille attacked not only Mairet the author, but his family and his background as well.[2] Mairet's subsequent defense of himself and his family in letters to such people as Georges de Scudéry, the true leader of the anti-Corneille group, gives valuable information about the author's early life and the beginning of his career. Although some circumspection is necessary when the author speaks about himself, the information provides a starting point for his biography.

Despite his arguments to the contrary during the quarrel, the origins of Mairet's family are evidently modest. Originally German inhabitants of Ormund in Westphalia, the Mairet family moved in the sixteenth century to Besançon, a city in the province of Franche-Comté and part of the Holy Roman Empire. Mairet's great-grandfather Gabriel initiated the move from Germany because of the increasing encroachment of Protestants in that region. An ardent and proud Catholic, he was anxious to hold to his religion and live in an area where his family could practice

Catholicism freely. Gabriel's son Jean, the poet's grandfather, distinguished himself in June, 1575, during an attack on Besançon by Swiss reformationist troops. Spurred no doubt by a combination of patriotism, religious ardor, and the simple desire to protect his family and property, he roused neighbors and aided in repulsing the attackers. For his bravery in the service of the city he was accorded the rank of sergeant-major in the militia, and given the right to display a coat of arms.[3]

Jean and his wife Catherine Fauche of Pontarlier had three sons. Two died at a relatively early age, one while studying in Louvain, Belgium, the other in the battle of Nuiport in 1600. The father intended their youngest son, also named Jean, to pursue a career in banking and commerce. Responding to Corneille's denigration of him as a petty bourgeois, Mairet took special care to explain this point in a letter addressed to Scudéry dated September 29, 1637.[4] Those of his family, Mairet stated, are all "Honnêtes gens," and the commercial trades do not debase those who exercise them. Taking as examples contemporary Italian and English families, he spoke of the honor of such a profession. Furthermore, the poet continued, although his father spent two years in Milan in order to learn cloth merchandising, he left the profession without ever having worked in it, because of an inheritance. Problems arose subsequently because of his father's wasteful spending, which ultimately resulted in the financial ruin of the family. Mairet thus justified his family's state of affairs while insisting that the far from prosperous situation did not indicate shameful origins.

In the same letter Mairet had much less difficulty establishing ties of nobility for his mother Marie Clerget, a woman from Troyes whose family was connected to the minor nobility of Champagne. Mairet's eagerness to relate himself to nobility arose not only from a common desire to elevate oneself socially but also in response to Corneille's claims that his own family was of higher social standing. The attitude of both authors is indicative of the seventeenth-century mentality, which sought to claim all possible connection with those of higher social station. In reality, despite the pretensions to nobility, both men most likely came from similar immediate family circumstances and were both bourgeois.

Mairet's Life

Although a nephew of the poet stated in a family memoir that Jean Mairet's birthdate was January 4, 1604,[5] it appears more probable that he was born in May of that year. His baptism took place on May 10,[6] and such a lapse of time between birth and baptism was unlikely in a profoundly Catholic family. The most probable date is May 9, because of the custom according to which a child received baptism the day immediately following its birth. His parents had four children, two sons and two daughters, and the mother died at an early age. After remarrying, Mairet's father also died, leaving the children in the care of a stepmother for whom Mairet apparently had no affection.

Before completing his education Mairet decided to leave Besançon for Paris. He stated that he was sixteen years of age at the time, and gave two reasons for the decision; the plague that ravaged the city and the similar departure of his friend Antoine Brun.[7] Clues to Mairet's early life can perhaps be drawn from the information known about Brun, with whom the poet remained friendly throughout his life. Originally from Dôle and four years older than Mairet, Antoine Brun studied with great application and apparent ease at the university in his home city. When in Paris he wrote some minor verse praised by such writers as Théophile de Viau, Guez de Balzac and Guillaume Colletet, of whom he was a great friend. Referring to his oratorical abilities Balzac even called him the Demosthenes of Dôle. Later he became *procureur général* of the province of Franche-Comté and ambassador to Holland. Although one can only speculate, it appears highly possible that in Besançon Mairet heard of his friend's success, literary and worldly, and decided to try his own chances. He apparently felt little holding him in his home city and realized that he had few possibilities there for the kind of acclaim that only Paris could offer.

II *Mairet and the duc de Montmorency*

While in Paris Mairet studied at the Collège des Grassins. Again, according to his own testimony, an outbreak of the plague forced him, in 1625, to leave Paris and travel south to Fontainebleau. He spoke in one poem of "la peste toujours sur mes pas" ("the plague constantly on my footsteps").[8] This trip may have been more a planned maneuver than simply a fortuitous jaunt, for the royal court was residing in Fontainebleau at the time. It was there that Mairet, in June or early July of 1625, met the duc de Montmorency, who took him into his service and thereby became Mairet's first protector.

In September of that year he accompanied Montmorency on an expedition against the rebelling army of Soubise and the Protestants at La Rochelle. Within the space of twelve days Mairet distinguished himself in two battles, one on land, the other at sea. He apparently received several wounds during the battle for the Isle de Ré, because he later dedicated a long ode to Bazan, the doctor who cured him when "the gravediggers of Ré were already marking the fatal spot where I should be buried."[9] For his bravery writers later compared him to Aeschylus, who, besides writing tragedies, fought valiantly in the battle of Marathon. Montmorency awarded Mairet a pension of fifteen hundred *livres*. After that time Mairet lived in the duke's chateau at Chantilly, possibly serving him as personal secretary.

Henri II, duc de Montmorency, godson of the late King Henri IV, was the most important protector of his day. The situation of the writers in his entourage illustrates what became the pattern for Mairet's life. In his *Historiettes* Tallemant des Réaux spoke of Montmorency and his artists. "He always had knowledgeable people in his service, who wrote verses for him, who kept him up on a million different subjects, and who told him how he should judge current topics of interest."[10] Montmorency did not enjoy the reputation of being among the most intelligent men of his day, but he did know his privileged role and played it well. Montmorency fashioned his life-style after the model set by Renaissance Italian princes. Artists and men of letters served them, living in the family residence, accompanying the protectors on various journeys and expeditions, glorifying them in works of art or literature. These works were to attest in later years to the splendor of the protectors' lives and exploits, as well as their culture and generosity in supporting the artists. Rich nobles granted employment of a minor sort to such men allowing them sufficent freedom for their creative work, and for which they received pensions. Mairet presents a typical case.

Mairet's Life

Specific instances of his pen's service to the protector include a long ode which he wrote about a naval battle in which Montmorency participated during the campaign of 1625. He praised the duke as immortal and described his deeds as veritable miracles.[11] The author also wrote a short poem about the Isle de Ré, which the duke besieged and freed from the English.

Mairet was not the only poet under the protection of the duc de Montmorency. Among others at Chantilly was Théophile de Viau, who had been freed from prison in September, 1625, although he did not rejoin the duke until April of the following year. The two poets formed a strong friendship, the influence of which shows clearly in Mairet's work. Sometime after Théophile's death in September, 1626, the duke entrusted Mairet with some works and letters of the late poet, which were published in 1641 as "Nouvelles Oeuvres de feu M. Théophile / Composées d'excellentes Lettres Françoises et Latines."

Because of Mairet's friendship with Théophile, problems arise concerning the exact date of composition of Mairet's first play, *Chryséide et Arimand*, a pastoral tragicomedy. Did he write it before or after his entrance into the service of Montmorency in mid-1625? Arguing for the latter possibility Antoine Adam states that the influence of Théophile and his play *Pyrame et Thisbé* is so pronounced in *Chryséide et Arimand* that Mairet could not have written it before September, 1625, when, according to all indications, the two poets met.[12] While the noted influence undeniably exists it is more literary than personal, growing from knowledge of the written text rather than from personal contact with the author. Théophile had published *Pyrame et Thisbé*, his celebrated tragedy, in 1623, according Mairet the opportunity to consult the play's printed text. The influence of Théophile on Mairet's second play, *Sylvie*, which he wrote when they both resided at Chantilly, is more complete, more striking. The presence of the older poet can almost be felt in certain passages, whereas the same is not true for the first play. Another argument for the earlier date of composition is Corneille's *Advertissement*, which spoke of the play as finished and presented to a company of actors before Mairet joined the duke.[13] Finally, Mairet must have enjoyed some reputation as an author or it is unlikely that Montmorency would have taken him into his service. Patrons rarely offered such recompense to writers who had not proved themselves worthy of the honor. It seems most probable therefore that Mairet's first play was both completed and performed before the author entered the service of the duc de Montmorency and met Théophile.

Critics of the time, especially those unfriendly to the author, saw more than the simple influence of Théophile on Mairet during the writing of *Sylvie*. Some claimed that the dying Théophile had entrusted Mairet with the work, and that Mairet subsequently presented the play as his own. This hypothesis has been proved false. There remains, however, the matter of one scene of the play published separately in 1627 under the title "Comédie ou dialogue de Philène et de Sylvie."[14] This dialogue of rhyming couplets between a lovesick young man and a witty shepherdess who refuses to cure his woes proved so popular that people still memorized and recited it many years after the initial success of the play.[15] According to some, this entire scene had come from Théophile's pen, and it remains difficult to prove absolutely the contrary. The influence of the older poet is most certainly strong, but stylistic indications point to Mairet's authorship rather than to that of Théophile. The most probable explanation is that some editor published the dialogue surreptitiously and without Mairet's knowledge shortly after the presentation of the play, because of the scene's enormous success as the actors delivered it on stage. The general rule for publication of plays at that time was that the authors would withhold the text until the end of the play's initial successful run in one theater, because after publication any company could stage the work without payment to the author. It was thus in his own interest to keep his work in the care of one theatrical troupe for as long as possible. But since publishers frequently pirated texts, as would happen in 1630 to Mairet's *Chryséide et Arimand*, the dialogue from *Sylvie* could have suffered the same fate. Bellerose's company performed both plays at the Hôtel de Bourgogne, but it is impossible to assign a specific date of creation to either play.

As both custom and courtesy dictated, Mairet dedicated *Sylvie*, published integrally in 1628, to his patron. He spoke of composing the play in the cool solitudes of the forest around Chantilly, where Théophile had earlier written his collection of odes "La Maison de Sylvie." In their poetry the two authors referred to the duchess as "Sylvie," and the duke as "Alcide." The dedication established quite clearly the protector-poet relationship, as Mairet spoke of the duke's love of literature extending to the establishment of pensions for writers. In a more personal note the poet expressed his gratitude for the duke's support of Théophile and for pleading his innocence.[16] Since Théophile had died in 1626, shortly after, or perhaps during, the writing of *Sylvie*, Mairet hoped in dedicating the play to Montmorency to fulfill a lasting debt of gratitude and express the appreciation of both men. Throughout the piece Mairet sustained a tone of ardent but almost humble sincerity and admiration for the duke's unceasing generosity. Montmorency's staunch defense of Théophile had touched Mairet profoundly. Through the duke's efforts the church permitted the poet's burial in consecrated ground, although an ecclesiastical court had earlier condemned Théophile as a heretic and a libertine.

Between the writing of *Sylvie* and *Silvanire*, his third play, Mairet underwent further influences in the literary world of Chantilly and Paris. Two men who exercised a particularly important influence on the poet, and consequently on the history of French theater, were Adrien de Montluc, comte de Carmail (alternately spelled Cramail), and Louis de Nogaret d'Epernon, cardinal de la Valette. Both men typified the nobles of the period who played an active role in literary circles. Carmail belonged to a group which attempted to combat the coarseness and bad taste rampant in the literature of that time. He himself wrote two comedies. The cardinal de la Valette was in close contact with Richelieu concerning literary matters. His unceasing devotion to "Son Eminence Rouge" earned him the nickname "le Cardinal Valet." In the preface to *Silvanire,* written in 1631 and directed to the comte de Carmail, Mairet explained the genesis of the work. Eager for French literature to approach the beauty and orderliness of the masterpieces of Italian literature, Carmail and La Valette had requested that the poet produce a work in imitation of the Italian dramatic pastorals.[17] *Silvanire,* probably performed in late 1629 or early 1630, thus found its origins in the express desire of two amateur literary men anxious to present before the French public a work that differed in structure and tone from those currently in fashion. The impetus did not come from the author himself but from those above him, again illustrating the basic role of the author in service to others. One can almost say that *Silvanire,* the first regular French dramatic pastoral and as such a sign of the classical unities' increasing importance, was a commissioned work.

The duc de Montmorency was executed in Toulouse on October 30, 1632, by orders of Louis XIII, behind whom Richelieu's hand could be felt. Montmorency was implicated in a plot with Gaston d'Orléans, the king's exiled brother, to overthrow Richelieu by force of arms. An ill-conceived, poorly timed maneuver, the plot resulted in the capture of Montmorency. Thus, in 1632 ended the first stage of Mairet's literary life as protected poet, although throughout his career he continued to speak of the duke in letters and dedications. Examination of those texts reveals Mairet's deep devotion to the memory of the duc de Montmorency.

Mairet mentioned Montmorency in the prefaces to four of his plays, although only one, *Sylvie,* was directly dedicated to him. The poet dedicated *Silvanire* to the duke's wife, Marie Félicie des Ursins, duchesse de Montmorency, in 1631 at a time when her husband was still alive. According to the poet he was "one of the most glorious men in the world."[18] Five years later in 1636 Mairet dedicated a play to Antoine Brun. In this dedication, four years after the death of the protector and at a time when Mairet was employed by the comte de Belin, he praised Montmorency as "the greatest, most magnificent, most glorious man of all those of his condition that France has ever borne, if we omit the last three months of his life with which all my hopes finally collapsed."[19] Mairet made final mention of Montmorency in the dedication to the duchess of the tragedy, *Le Grand et dernier Solyman,* dated 1639. Her husband, whom she rightly mourned, was "le plus brave, le plus généreux, le plus libéral, le plus vaillant en un mot le plus aymable et le plus accomply Héros" ("the bravest, most generous, most liberal, most valiant—in a word the kindest and most accomplished hero").[20] Such panegyrics, though certainly expected from one in Mairet's position, go far beyond the necessity of showing gratitude for benefits accrued in the duke's employment. Mairet felt strong personal attachment to his protector and was sincerely moved by his high ideals. Although hardly in a position to criticize the highest powers of the realm, Mairet seems never to have forgiven Louis XIII and especially Richelieu for what many people believed an unnecessarily harsh judgment of such a great man. Mairet showed courage in never forgetting his lasting debt to the man in whose house he first developed his literary talents.

III Mairet, the comte de Belin, and the Quarrel of the Cid

Almost immediately after the death of Montmorency, Mairet entered the service of François d'Averton, comte de Belin, who already protected Rotrou, Scudéry, Scarron, Montdory, and the troupe of the Théâtre du Marais. Scarron in *Le Roman Comique* depicted Belin as the comte d'Orsé, a gentleman enamored of the theater, who every year brought the best acting companies to Le Mans. Having lost favor at court in 1620 as a result of quarrels between the king and the queen mother, Belin retired to his lands in the province of Maine. He sojourned often in Le Mans, where a literary circle of some importance existed. In an apparent reference to Mairet and Rotrou, La Pinelière in *Parnasse* said of Belin that "he has in his house two of the brightest and most eloquent Muses who appear in the theater."[21] Mairet remained in the count's service for six years until Belin's death in 1638.

In the *Historiettes* Tallemant discussed an interesting aspect of Mairet's service to the count, which furthers consideration of the poet's role as willing scribe to the protector's desires. According to this story Belin was enamored of Mlle le Noir, the leading lady of Montdory's company at the Théâtre du Marais, and instructed Mairet to write plays in which she would act the principal role.[22] Since Mlle le Noir and her husband left the

Marais for the rival Hôtel de Bourgogne on the king's orders in 1634, according to Tallemant she created the heroines of *les Galanteries du duc d'Ossonne, Virginie,* and *Sophonisbe,* written by Mairet between 1632 and 1634 and performed at the Théâtre du Marais when she was the company's principal actress. Though founded on a kernel of truth there entered some measure of disparagement in the story. Mlle le Noir was not the sole reason for the count's interest in Montdory's troupe, and he continued the protection even after the leading actress left the company. The count's machinations for the actors went beyond simply furnishing plays in which they could display their talents. On occasion he even supplied the theater, thereby aiding in the establishment of the company's reputation. Again, according to Tallemant, he prevailed upon the marquise de Rambouillet to allow a performance of Mairet's *Virginie* in her home.[23] Belin was a good friend of the marquise's husband, another of the principal residents of Le Maine, and such a favor was easily granted. Furthering his own design, whatever it may have been, the comte de Belin succeeded in advancing his poet also.

A short remark by Segrais in the *Segraisiana* mentioned the composition of *Sophonisbe,* Mairet's first tragedy, in 1634. According to Segrais, Chapelain first examined the unity of time, the twenty-four-hour rule. He communicated his interest to Mairet, who then wrote *Sophonisbe,* which Segrais called the first play that observed the rule.[24] Should Segrais' remark be true, the impetus behind the writing of Mairet's tragedy belonged not to the author but to the scholar and theoretician Chapelain, who originally conceived the idea. The situation finds a perfect parallel in Mairet's role in the creation of *Silvanire,* that of the author who took a suggestion from a person of higher authority, then fashioned it into a literary work. Mairet and Chapelain were in contact at that time, the poet acting as an intermediary between Chapelain in Paris and Belin in Le Mans.

Also of note is Segrais' remark that the actors hesitated before accepting the play, perhaps because they feared there would be no audience interest in a work which, through stricter application of the unifying rules, lacked the rebounding action of the tragicomedy, the most popular genre. They reportedly acquiesced under pressure from the comte de Fiesque. The troupe of the Théâtre du Marais first performed *Sophonisbe* in the fall of 1634. Despite the anxieties of the actors the play proved extremely popular both with the literary men and with the general public. It remained one of Mairet's two greatest successes, and with justifiable pride he stated in the dedication that his play had "drawn sighs from the greatest hearts and tears from the most beautiful eyes in France."[25] The tragedy's triumph in aristocratic circles is seen by the fact that it was performed in 1636 at the Hôtel de Rambouillet by Julie d'Angennes, daughter of the marquise, and by friends of her mother.

The six years during which Mairet served the comte de Belin represent the central part of the author's career. In that period he wrote seven plays, including works in all the dramatic genres of the time, ranging from pastoral to comedy to tragedy to tragicomedy. He reached the height of his glory, and after the success of *Sophonisbe* in 1634 critics and the public alike acclaimed him the leading dramatic poet in France. *Sophonisbe,* the sixth of his twelve plays, marks the midpoint of his career, and the apogee of his standing in the eyes of the public. With his following endeavors he never succeeded in repeating his great accomplishment or in winning the adulation of theatrical audiences. With his next two tragedies Mairet found himself in direct competition with authors writing plays based on the same stories. Dalibray's *Soliman,* performed at the Théâtre du Marais in 1635, prevented the production during the same year of Mairet's *Solyman,* which the troupe of the Hôtel de Bourgogne finally staged in 1637–38. The two companies performed Mairet's *Marc Antoine* and Benserade's *Cléopâtre* in 1635–36, the former with Montdory at the Marais, the latter at the Hôtel de Bourgogne. They seem to have garnered equal success, despite Corneille's claims that his rival's play was "buried" by that of Benserade.[26]

The famous quarrel of the *Cid* began in February of 1637 after the triumph of *Le Cid* and lasted until October of that year, with letters and pamphlets flying, tempers and passions burning. Scudéry and Mairet were the most virulent in their attacks against Corneille, with Mairet growing increasingly bitter as Corneille denigrated not only his literary works but also his family background and birthplace. Rather than a scholarly discussion of literary principles, the quarrel between Mairet and Corneille remained on a strictly personal level. Before the incidents the two men had been good friends, and Mairet had offered a poem in honor of Corneille's comedy *La Veuve* in 1634. At that time Mairet enjoyed great favor and was about to achieve his most outstanding success. In 1637 he could hardly have considered Corneille serious competition for the highest literary rank, which Mairet thought belonged to him. Frustrated by the lack of renewed public acclaim since the presentation of *Sophonisbe* three years earlier, he must have been particularly vulnerable to attacks, and his pride suffered the consequences. The excesses of Mairet's vituperations must be seen as the result of his own disappointment as well as Corneille's pointed barbs, since the latter managed to hit Mairet's sorest spots. Among other interesting notes one learns from Corneille that Mairet was nicknamed "Innocent le Bel" by the actors. In a reference to Mairet's birth in Franche-Comté Corneille said: "He was not born French, so we must excuse the mistakes he continuously makes against the language."[27]

During the quarrel Mairet spent the majority of his time in Le Mans, leading Corneille to state that Mairet owed the greatest part of his reputation to the protection and benevolence of the comte de Belin. Since Belin protected Scudéry as well as Mairet, Corneille knew well where the attacks originated. Rotrou, also a part of Belin's entourage, apparently took the role of conciliator, anxious to end the quarrel and reunite men who were previously friends. Finally on October 5, 1637, Boisrobert, under orders from Richelieu, wrote to Mairet at Le Mans to put an end to the war of pamphlets and insults.

Mairet was left more than slightly wounded by the quarrel. Corneille had forced him to recite his entire family tree in defense against the slanderous remarks, and Mairet was unable to produce the only possibly adequate offense—a play that would receive greater public acclaim than *Le Cid*.

His next two plays, *l'Illustre Corsaire* and *Roland Furieux* were tragicomedies, both written in 1637 and performed at the Hôtel de Bourgogne during the 1637–38 season. Neither proved a great success, although *l'Illustre Corsaire* was performed at Rueil

Mairet's Life

with the approbation of Cardinal Richelieu. Mairet dedicated the play to Madame la duchesse d'Aiguillon, the cardinal's niece. The author obviously intended the dedication as a means of gaining favors from her illustrious and powerful uncle.

Mairet's ties to his second protector, the comte de Belin, were definitely less marked and less personal than his strong relationship with Montmorency. Although in his service since 1632 the author waited until 1637 to dedicate one of his works, the tragedy *Marc Antoine*, to his protector. Under some criticism for this apparent lack of gratitude, Mairet hastened to explain that he had waited in order to present the count with the one of his plays that he esteemed the highest.[28] The excuse rings somewhat false, for Mairet habitually expressed preference for his current work. He apparently felt little personal need for an outward show of appreciation, indicating perhaps some distance between himself and Belin. In the 1636 dedication of *les Galanteries*, the first play that Mairet wrote during his service to Belin, he included a short remark indicative of the poet-protector relationship between the two men. Mairet mentioned that the count "adds to the benefits that he gives me, my liberty."[29] As an author who needed his time and freedom to write, Mairet was justifiably appreciative of the atmosphere in which he had the good fortune to work. He noted in the 1637 dedication of *Marc Antoine* that Belin's house was a shelter where "I peacefully enjoy the rest and the calm necessary to the Muses."[30] What Mairet praised was the count's attitude toward him, his goodness and generosity, rather than the count himself and his own exploits and deeds. The comte de Belin was not Henri II de Montmorency, and Mairet's attitude toward him was more businesslike in comparison to his great respect and continuing devotion to the earlier protector.

Mairet did not, however, lack the necessary external show of respect. Having played the role of protected author for some thirteen years he knew very well the proper attitude and the expected mode of conduct. Belin died on September 29, 1638. Some time after the funeral Chapelain wrote Mairet praising him "for the resolution you made to pay him final respects and to accompany the body to the graveside."[31] In the same letter Chapelain mentioned Mairet's continuing progress on *Athénaïs*, the poet's eleventh work, which was to be performed at the Hôtel de Rambouillet. Having completed ten plays and in the process of writing another, Mairet lost the support of his second protector. He did not immediately forget the late count's generosity, however, for he dedicated *Roland Furieux*, published two years after the count's death, to his son. The dedication contained warm praise for the man in whose employment Mairet spent six years. He mentioned that the count had a special fondness for the source of the play, Ariosto's *Orlando Furioso*,[32] and it is likely that the count suggested the subject of the play to the poet.

Athénaïs, written in 1638 and published in 1642, was dedicated to Emeric Marc de la Ferté, Bishop of Le Mans, in whose house Mairet had spent four or five months after the death of Belin. Being an important personage in the province and the city, Belin had close contacts with the men of the church, and through him Mairet also came into their circle of interest.

Mairet composed his final dramatic poem, *Sidonie*, his fourth tragicomedy after the succession of three tragedies, while residing in Le Mans. Before its stage presentation he read it aloud to Marie de Hautefort, a former lady-in-waiting to the queen, who, with her sister, had been banished from the court by Queen Anne d'Autriche to live in Le Mans. Mairet dedicated the play to Mlle de Hautefort. It was with this play that, in 1640, Jean Mairet abandoned writing for the stage. In the "Au lecteur" preceding *Sidonie*, written three years after the decision, Mairet stated his reasons. He wanted to write more serious works "whose success would depend less on the opinion or mood of an audience, where voices are counted rather than weighed, and less on the disposition of the Actors, of whom the majority assume the characters that please them rather than playing the roles for which they are suited."[33] Despite this decision to leave theatrical writing for more serious works Mairet wrote nothing more. He had lost favor with the public, being unable to repeat the success of *Sophonisbe*. He likewise fell out with the actors, again because of the less than mediocre responses to his most recent plays. In the final evaluation success depended upon audience reception, and it had been a long time since Mairet had received the satisfaction of public acclaim. His works no longer appealed to an audience whose tastes had changed, while the author himself had not.

Throughout his career Mairet necessarily came in contact with Cardinal Richelieu, the most important and influential protector of the times. Mairet was most definitely not one of those admitted to Richelieu's inner circle. He rarely addressed the cardinal directly, approaching him through his secretary Boisrobert or Chapelain or others, such as the cardinal's niece. The main reason for Mairet's outside position lies in his earlier protection by Montmorency, whose death Richelieu had precipitated. Others in the duke's circle, though not all, remained hostile to the power of the cardinal. The comte de Carmail, attached to the Prince de Condé, a nephew of Montmorency, and earlier a member of the duke's circle, was intermittently involved in plots to force Louis XIII to dismiss the cardinal. He was finally imprisoned in the Bastille from 1630 to 1642. There must have been some measure of hesitation and suspicion on the parts of both Mairet and Richelieu. The author did not participate in any of the theatrical group efforts sanctioned by the cardinal or Boisrobert, though he did periodically receive benefits.

After the termination of the quarrel of the *Cid*, Mairet wrote to Chapelain in December, 1637, imploring his services in procuring some aid from the cardinal. Two weeks later Chapelain informed Mairet that through the intercession of Boisrobert the cardinal had granted him "six cent francs en pistoles." Boisrobert reputedly had told the cardinal that because of *Sylvie*, a play that was particularly appreciated by the female public, all the women would bless him for having the goodness to help "poor Mairet." In his letter to Mairet, Chapelain added a curious note. "Il est superflu d'avertir un aussy bon Courtisan que vous qu'il sera de la bienséance d'en escrire un mot de civilité à ce favorable agent des Muses." (It is unnecessary to warn such a good man of the courts as you that it would be fitting to write a note of gratitude to this kind agent of the Muses.)[34] Chapelain succinctly defined Mairet's place in the life of the times. Like many authors who lacked sufficient funds to allow them to live by literature alone, he was a courtesan—one who paid court to others and who received remuneration from them. His life was not entirely his own, and at times he found it necessary to request sustenance from those in a position to provide it. It was an accepted role in the society, and Mairet occupied it with great success from 1625 to 1638.

IV *Life after Literature*

Mairet held to his resolution not to write any more plays, but in 1641 he did edit and publish the papers of Théophile with which Montmorency had entrusted him. He dedicated the volume to Richelieu begging the cardinal's pardon for his inability to present a work of his own pen, as Mairet put it, "since nature has refused me the means of thanking you with my own works."[35]

In July, 1647, Mairet married Jeanne de Cardouan, daughter of Jacques de Cardouan and a member of an established family from lower Maine, and returned with her to Paris. She died eleven years later having borne no children. Less than one year after Mairet's marriage, in January, 1648, the Baron de Scey, military governor of Franche-Comté, proposed him as a diplomatic agent of his native province to the French court at Paris. Having lived in France since the early 1620s and being an established person with ties to influential circles, Mairet was a logical choice for the mission. At stake were both the neutrality and the tranquility of the province, as it could easily have become a battleground between France and the German principalities. The first treaty was drawn up and signed March 3, 1649, by Mairet and the Maréchal de Villeroy, with the Prince de Condé as intermediary. They established a second more permanent treaty of neutrality with much difficulty on September 25, 1651. The problem during the drafting of the new treaty grew from a general mistrust of the province and of Mairet, its principal negotiator, on the part of the French. In the late 1640s Condé had played an essential role in the Fronde of the Princes, and his uncle was Mairet's first protector. Furthermore, it seems not unlikely that Mairet showed some sympathy for the Fronde.

In 1654 the emperor of the Holy Roman Empire decided to name Mairet permanent resident of the empire to the court of France, but shortly thereafter Mazarin banished him from the country. He had reputedly defended the honor of the King of Spain whom Mazarin had accused of welcoming Condé to Spain only in order to betray him later. Mairet left Paris and settled in Besançon. In September, 1668, he received his letters of nobility from the Emperor Leopold and could sign himself Jean de Mairet. His pride, bandied about during the bitter quarrel with Corneille, forced him to refer to them as his "new" letters, since he never admitted that the nobility did not date from further back in the family tree. After returning to Besançon he visited Paris only once. Although he outlived his old nemesis Corneille and saw the evolution of French theater from the early pastoral and tragicomedy to the classical tragedy, he played no literary role for the last forty-six years of his life. At the age of eighty-one he died in Besançon on January 31, 1686.

CHAPTER 2

First Attempts and First Success

I Introduction: the State of Theater in 1625

THE first third of the seventeenth century, in particular the years of the 1620s and 1630s, marked the triumph of what critics called the irregular genres. The term designated above all tragicomedy but also dramatic pastoral and the hybrid variation of the two, the pastoral tragicomedy. In reaction to the static quality of sixteenth-century tragedy, the irregular genres found their origins in the less limited contemporary dramatic form, the *drame libre*. Disregarding the unifying elements or characteristics of the humanistic tragedy, they emphasized variety, diversity of effects, and complication in plot line designed to hold the audience interest. Theater abandoned the concerns of earlier scholarly critics, in favor of confrontation with a new theatrical audience, one which was eager to be surprised by adventures it could see only on stage. For this reason, the emphasis shifted from lyrical beauty to visual effects, from static monologues to dialogue, finally from poetry to action. The only unifying feature sought or demanded was the unity of interest provided by a continuing plot line, with complications and reversals readily accepted, or by the adventures of a protagonist, alone or part of a group. Representative of this period of change, Alexandre Hardy played a role of major importance in creating an audience-oriented theater.[1] As a *poète à gages* ("salaried playwright") engaged to a theatrical company he had direct experience with both actors and audience, and his theater reflects the adaptation process of the dramatic genres to the tastes and desires of the public.

In the early part of the century the most popular dramatic genre was the tragicomedy.[2] Although late sixteenth and early seventeenth century audiences saw tragicomedies with Biblical plots, as well as others based on *moralités* or mystery plays, the largest number were of novelistic inspiration. Garnier's *Bradamante*, written in 1582, fixed the genre. Based on an episode from Ariosto's *Orlando Furioso*, the play told a fictitious tale of amorous intrigue, alternating tragic tirades with scenes of comedy and concluding with a happy ending. The tragicomedies of Hardy, of which thirteen are extant, increased the popularity of the genre. They belong to several different types—mythological, historical, neoclassical, bourgeois. Hardy followed Garnier's example in abolishing the chorus, realizing that this remnant from lyrical tragedy burdened the tragicomic stage by slowing the action and dissipating interest. He was especially important for his role in bringing about the necessary evolution of drama toward action, often including scenes of violence rather than permitting such exciting events to be related by a messenger. In general, however, Hardy's tragicomedies are differentiated from his tragedies only by their happy endings. Although in great part responsible for the immense success of the genre and for liberating it from the limiting conventions of earlier drama, he still belonged to the older tradition in means of expression, inspiration, and dramatic form.

The great vogue of the tragicomedy began in the late 1620s with a new generation of writers. Reacting against the outmoded theater of Hardy, such authors as Du Ryer, Mareschal, Pichou, and Mairet created the "new" tragicomedy and ensured its domination of the French stage, culminating in the immense popular success of the most well known French tragicomedy *Le Cid* (1636–37). The strength of the irregular genre and the interest which it stimulated both in the authors and in the public are evidenced by Jean de Schelandre's reworking of his own *Tyr et Sidon*. Having originally presented the play as a tragedy in 1608, the author rewrote it as a tragicomedy of *deux journées* in 1628. François Ogier's preface, a staunch defense of the *drame libre* and the irregular genres which had derived from it, presented a justification for forsaking the old genre in favor of the new.

For source material the authors of tragicomedies limited themselves to novelistic literature, renouncing the more varied sources in which Hardy found his inspiration. The stories dramatized were fictitious, not historical, coming from Spanish tales and Italian novellas, as well as from French novelistic literature with d'Urfé's *l'Astrée*. True to the dualistic nature of the very name "tragicomedy," some mixture of tragic and comic elements was present, but in general the comedy was of lesser importance. The authors placed great emphasis on action and adventures rather than characterization or portrayal of finely analyzed sentiments. This particular characteristic evolved, however, under the influence of the pastoral and the desires of a more cultured public to see the portrayal of true human emotions rather than sheer unbridled violence or passion. The ending of the tragicomedy was always happy and usually resulted from simple exterior circumstances rather than from the characters' own feelings. The Cornelian dilemma and the dramatic possibilities of conflicting passions had not yet reached the heart of the tragicomedy.

The major objection to the theater of Hardy, and consequently the area in which the younger authors appeared the freshest by comparison, concerned the means of expression, the style of the dramatic writing. Throughout his career and in all genres Hardy proved himself a follower of the humanistic tradition. As time progressed, tastes changed; the younger authors realized this full well and wished to create works which would respond to those changes, thus creating a more modern dramatic spirit. Théophile's tragedy *Pyrame et Thisbé* (1621) had showed the way.[3] Although by virtue of its form the play is a product of older dramatic techniques, its tone and style, the expression of sentiments and ideas, are modern. Equally important in this respect was Racan's dramatic pastoral *Arthénice ou les Bergeries*.[4] But the creation of a new dramatic style was not merely a desire to create something different in reaction to that which had preceded. The role of the audience[5] rose to a position of prime importance, given the situation that theater, the most public of literary genres, must at all times be cognizant of the whims, fancies, and desires of its spectators. Especially after 1630 the composition of the theatrical public underwent a change. *Honnêtes gens* (well-bred people) began to replace the rowdy crowds of the *parterre*, the large open area directly in front of the stage where the less educated, less refined public massed.

First Attempts and First Success

The bourgeois and merchants, who were to pride themselves on attending every premiere of a given year, soon formed the nucleus of the theatrical audience. Women likewise went to the theater with more liberty, daring to appear unmasked.[6] The force of their influence is not to be overlooked.

Tragicomedy's main rival for public attention and acclamation was the pastoral,[7] a genre which almost equaled the tragicomedy in popularity before finally dying out in the 1630s. As a literary genre the dramatic pastoral arrived in France fully created, being the product of two foreign influences before it became truly French. Italian literature exercised the greatest influence, with Guarini's *Pastor fido* and Tasso's *Aminta* of most interest. Both works had been translated into French by the end of the sixteenth century and had served as sources for French dramatic pastorals as early as 1600. The other foreign influence, of somewhat less importance, was Spanish novelistic literature, exemplified in *La Diana* by Montemayor. The incursion of Spanish dramatic techniques and themes into French literature reflected a vogue for that country in the first years of the century. From the Italian sources the French learned to appreciate analysis of sentiments and passions, and they came to understand the dramatic utility of portraying emotions. Spanish literature provided action and movement, proving especially important for stage presentation of the pastoral. Through the portrayal of inner sentiment supported by exterior reality and stage movement sufficient to sustain interest, the two currents combined and completed each other.

Hardy's pastorals were in general of the same spirit as his tragicomedies, although he tempered the violence of passion and action characteristic of the latter genre for proper portrayal of emotions. Honoré d'Urfé proved to be the author who truly made the pastoral French, and in doing so he provided an all but limitless source of plots for both dramatic pastorals and tragicomedies with his novel *l'Astrée*.[8] The adventures and philosophical discussion on the nature of love no longer took place in a conventional idyllic Arcadia, but in a specific corner of France. Despite the seemingly endless nature of the story which fills five volumes, d'Urfé showed a care for order and clarity, and a concern for verisimilitude which separated his work from the fantastic quality of the Italian pastorals. Of major importance for the theater, d'Urfé's work gave the pastoral the possibility of becoming truly dramatic. With the emphasis on the human values of the stories, the characterization and psychology of the characters and the conflicts of passion which they suffered, the author broke necessary ground for dramatic adaptations which would go beyond simple romantic tales of unrequited love and lyrical suffering.

D'Urfé's influence on the theater was not immediate, however. The first dramatic pastoral of any importance to appear at the time, *Les Bergeries* by Racan, published in 1625, reverted to the nature of the Italian sources, with emphasis on elegance of expression, precision and nobility in the dialogue. Racan, nonetheless, did play a role in ridding the pastoral of unnecessary elements by his rejection of mythological and purely chivalric aspects. His influence, not solely in the pastoral genre, was primarily in the area of style.

The true nature of the pastoral, dramatic or novelistic, differed essentially from that of the tragicomedy. Whereas the tragicomedy existed primarily as a dramatic portrait of action, the realm of the pastoral was poetry. The emotions it portrayed were less violent, nobler, and perhaps more civilized, and their expression more gracious. With its introduction into French theater, the pastoral ceased being the pastime of small circles of literary elite and addressed itself to the public in general. For this reason it began to participate in the nature of the tragicomedy, adding movement and action to its dialogues in order to attain and please the larger audience. Descriptive lyric poetry remained a necessary element as the characters extolled love as "honest friendship" and proclaimed life in the country preferable to the rigors of the city. The authors often included purely lyrical poetic forms in their plays as prologues or as choruses between the acts. These Italianate elements disappeared with Hardy, making few appearances in later plays.

As did the poetry of the pastoral, the characters followed certain well-defined patterns. They were shepherds and shepherdesses, more often disguised aristocrats enjoying the calm of the country than people who truly watched sheep as their livelihood. One personage who played a constant role was the magician.

First Attempts and First Success

He was the human representative of unknown supernatural forces at play in the lives of the characters.

Another necessary character in the earlier pastorals was the Satyr, the incarnation of carnal passion and the quest for sensual pleasures. Because of a desire to create a more human character, one who would not shock social mores as readily as the grotesque, bawdy satyr, Hylas came into being as the personification of amorous inconstancy.

Oracles, dreams, use of magic potions or spells, sudden recognitions by means of birthmarks or a bracelet worn since childhood can be found throughout the pastoral. Along with these various artificial devices the role played by pure chance was very great, underlying the general lack of necessary subordination of dramatic action to the characters. Important progress was still to be made in unifying the plot and its movement with the characters and their psychology.

The most essential element of the pastoral, that which animated both its poetry and its plot, was the portrayal of love. Serious in the Platonic fashion, love was virtuous and elevated almost to the point of being a god. As love commanded the actions of the characters and dictated their emotional being, the shepherds and shepherdesses spent long hours analyzing their sentiments or debating fine points of the Neoplatonic philosophy of love. Hylas argued for the pleasures of the chase and multiple conquests, while Céladon's entire being was defined by his constancy to the beloved Astrée.

From the inevitable marriage of tragicomedy and the pastoral arose a truly hybrid genre, the pastoral tragicomedy, which enjoyed some measure of popular success during the same period. It was representative of the loss of pure dramatic form, being the meeting point of several distinct earlier traditions as they merged into one conglomerate genre. Pure tragedy and pure comedy had both disappeared, losing their individual identity in the tragicomedy. The pure lyric pastoral combined with that irregular genre to form a new dramatic form, the pastoral tragicomedy. The baroque aesthetic of diversity and variation as the source of beauty reached an apogee in the mere name of the form.[9]

This period, the one in which Mairet wrote his first plays,

was an epoch of transition. Authors sought new inspiration and new forms of dramatic presentation in response to their own desires as well as those of a new public. The works written at this time represent the attempts of young, relatively inexperienced authors to create a new style, a modern style in line with the various foreign influences rather than the works of traditional French theater. When Mairet said that he would rather have written Tasso's *Aminta* than all the plays of Hardy, more than six hundred according to the author himself, he expressed the desire of his generation to establish a theater which would replace the old dramatic forms, infusing life into the art and renewing it in the eyes of the public.

II Chryséide et Arimand

The first of more than thirty tragicomedies and pastorals inspired by d'Urfé's *l'Astrée*, Mairet's first play, *Chryséide et Arimand*,[10] was performed in 1625.[11] The success of the play provided impetus for the growing influence of the novel on the theater, especially in the area of the portrayal of emotions. Earlier authors utilized emotion in their plays as a mere vehicle, relegating passion to the rank of dramatic utility. The general effect of Mairet's influence following *Chryséide et Arimand* was to temper the earlier theatrical extravagance and move toward a more realistic presentation of sentiments dependent on the psychology of the characters, who thus gained in credibility, as did the play as a whole. Although Mairet's initial theatrical endeavor shows touches of unrealistic exaggeration, it proved nonetheless influential, following the examples both of d'Urfé and of Théophile, in moving theater toward a more believable portrayal of human sentiments.

Another area in which *Chryséide et Arimand* exercised important influence functions as the necessary counterpart to the realm of human feelings and psychology. The play served to orient theater toward action in accord with those sentiments.[12] Action must be understood in a broad sense to mean not merely stage movement, which was not at all lacking in earlier tragicomedies, but also such elements as concentration of

First Attempts and First Success

interest, preparation, and suspense derived from the author's manipulation of the events. Movement for its own sake and emotion for its own sake were twin pitfalls awaiting authors who lacked the dramatic sense to avoid them. The interdependence of psychology and plot provided an essential step in the creation of the truly cohesive, unified drama of later French classicism. The transitional period of the late 1620s saw the first plays by authors who came to understand the necessity of this marriage of character to action, and during the first half of his career Mairet was to prove himself the most important among them.

Mairet seems to have had an innate dramatic sense, a feeling for what would succeed in stage presentation, which is evident in his very first play. A comparison of the plot of *Chryséide et Arimand* with its immediate source, an episode from *l'Astrée*, shows this understanding of action and the necessity of dramatizing events rather than relating them.

The story of Cryséide and Arimant (the spelling of the names differs in the novel) appears in the seventh and eighth books of the third part of *l'Astrée*, published in 1619. The various adventures of the two lovers are recounted to the assembled company first by Hylas, then by Florice, who had originally heard them from Cryséide herself. As stated by the narrators at the outset, the story will serve to demonstrate the power of "la fortune," meaning the seemingly capricious whims of chance, the stronger force of fate, and, above all, the power of the gods to determine the course of events affecting human lives. Born to the richest family in the province, Cryséide possessed all the charms that beauty and merit could provide. A druid priestess predicted, however, that such gifts would cause her misfortune. Arimant, her equal in moral worth as well as in physical attributes, fell in love with her at first sight, and after a short while she permitted him to believe that she returned his love. Although she refused a ring which Arimant offered, she promised to marry him if she could win her parents' consent.

As misfortune joins its bitterness to their joy, the heroine's mother decides to marry her to someone else. Cryséide is sent to the court of Rithimer, the one place forbidden to Arimant because of enmity between Rithimer and the hero's father. Having decided to kill herself rather than be forced into an unwelcome marriage, Cryséide has herself bled by two doctors. She unbinds her wounds after their departure and is about to bleed to death when her servant Clarine discovers her. In despair the girl sends news to Arimant of the death of his beloved. Upon receiving the message, Arimant decides to commit suicide himself after killing Clorange, one of Rithimer's retainers, whom Cryséide was to marry. On the road, however, he encounters the messenger sent to announce Cryséide's recovery. Disguised as a cloth merchant, he arrives in the city where she is living and manages to enter her chambers, where they plan their escape. Eventually they make their way to the house of Arimant's father, and Cryséide, disguised as a man, convinces him to allow his son to marry a virtuous maiden named Cryséide. The two lovers leave, purportedly in order to bring her back, but again fortune lets fall one of its blows. The city in which they are temporarily residing is attacked, defeated, and ravaged by Gondebaut, king of the Bourguignons. Along with all the women Cryséide and Clarine are taken prisoner. Arimant, wounded while trying to rally the citizens to the defense of their city, is left for dead.

At the beginning of the eighth book, Cryséide, held prisoner by Gondebaut in Lyon, learns from Bellaris, Arimant's servant, that Arimant is still alive. He was taken captive by Bellimart, who is holding him for a large ransom. The servant manages to help the two women escape, and after long rides at night they stop at an inn where Cryséide is to wait until Bellaris can arrange Arimant's escape. Once arrived at his master's prison, from which he was allowed to leave in order to press Arimant's father for the ransom, Bellaris announces his escape plan. He and Arimant will simply exchange clothes, and the guards will allow Arimant, dressed as the servant, to leave once again in quest of the money. Although the hero protests that he will do nothing which might endanger the life of his friend, Bellaris easily convinces him of the necessity of the move. Arimant thus escapes, and since Bellaris is adept enough to devise his own escape, they both arrive at the inn where Cryséide is waiting.

First Attempts and First Success 37

While the four are traveling the next day, however, Bellaris learns that Bellimart, searching for Arimant, is staying in the very inn they have chosen for the night. The men and the women separate after agreeing to meet in Vienne the next day. As misfortune would have it, the path of Cryséide crosses that of Gondebaut, who has been searching for her, and she is once again a prisoner. Since Bellaris was a witness to the expected capture, he informs his master, exhorting him to flee to Italy and forget Cryséide, since her womanly ambition to be a queen will doubtless destroy her love for the unfortunate Arimant. The hero refuses to be swayed by his servant's talk of feminine frivolity and women's love of honors. Having received a letter from Cryséide assuring him of her undying affection, he travels on to Lyon.

That day, as he and Bellaris arrive in the city, a great sacrifice is performed at the Tomb of the Two Lovers in order to bring about a change of heart in Cryséide, so that she will willingly accept the king as her husband. Instead, she seizes the sacrificial knife and running to the sacred tomb announces her resolution to kill herself rather than be forced to marry. She says it is the gods' will that she love another. Caught between his desire to have Cryséide and his fear of desecrating a holy place, thereby angering the gods and the people if he forces her from her protected shelter, the king is about to move toward her as the priests raise their objections. Suddenly Arimant arrives and announces that he knows the one who brought about Cryséide's escape. In an earlier proclamation the king had promised to grant one wish to the person who would give such information. Arimant announces that he is the guilty party and asks for Cryséide's liberty in exchange. No sooner has Gondebaut commanded that Cryséide be freed and Arimant bound than Bellaris arrives in his turn and declares that he, not Arimant, is truly the one who devised and executed the escape. Confused, astonished, and finally overwhelmed with admiration, the king orders that all be freed, stating that human wisdom is folly compared with that of the god whom they adore.

In writing the play, Mairet chose that section of the story which both contains the greatest part of the action and leads most quickly to the immediate crisis and resolution. The rest is either related as exposition or forgotten. Of the first half of the story, found in the seventh book, he retains the situation of the two lovers whose parents originally opposed their union, and he includes their flight, capture, and imprisonment in different cities. The complications involving Rithimer and his enmity toward the family of the hero, the marriage plans for Chryséide, and her attempted suicide are dropped. The action of the play follows the plot line developed in the eighth book, with substitutions of dialogues for monologues, fully developed scenes in place of short *récits* in *l'Astrée*, and many minor points of the story dropped. Although directly inspired by *l'Astrée*, Mairet's play ends by resembling Théophile's tragedy *Pyrame et Thisbé* in many respects. Common points between the two plays include the opposition of parents, the lovers' flight, and fate's usual persecution of innocent victims. It seems not unlikely that Mairet chose this particular episode of *l'Astrée* because of the story's similarity to Théophile's tragedy.

The entire first act of *Chryséide et Arimand* is a lengthy development by Mairet of minor episodes in the novel. In scene 1 two soldiers, Bellimard and Alexandre, pledge abiding friendship despite the current vice of treachery, and Alexandre promises to guard Bellimard's prisoner, a Segusien. The second scene opens with a long monologue delivered by Arimand about the misfortunes of fate. He is then joined by his servant, Bellaris, and they plan the servant's escape. Chryséide, the imprisoned heroine, begins the second act with a lyric monologue which is the perfect parallel to that of Arimand, whom she believes dead. Her servant, Clarinde, who may be considered one of the first *suivantes* (a combination maid and confidante) to appear on the French stage,[13] attempts to dissuade her from her black mood, as Bellaris arrives with the news that Arimand is very much alive. Together the two servants work out details of the escape. The monologue is of Mairet's invention, but with the arrival of Bellaris the play follows quite closely the plot line of the novel.

An important modification brought by Mairet to d'Urfé's story is the creation of more important roles for the servants. From minor, all but nameless figures, the playwright has drawn truly human characters and imbued them with wit and prosaic common sense, which contrast strikingly with the static attitudes of their masters. The latter couple remains closer to the prototypes of the pastorals and *l'Astrée*, existing as immobile beings given to self-pity and carried along by the actions, decisions and plans of others. Chryséide and Arimand admit that they live and breathe only by their servants. Bellaris and Clarinde present much more dramatic figures. They provide the necessary action to ensure that their masters not remain petrified in their lyricism, and in doing so they prevent the stagnation and loss of audience interest that would result from pure poetry on stage. Mairet's comprehension of the necessity of dramatic movement in character and plot is well evidenced by the creation of these two realistic characters.

The second scene of the second act introduces the audience to another character whose role Mairet has improved, the king Gondebaut. The very portrait of royal pride and conceit, the king owes a great deal to Théophile's king in *Pyrame et Thisbé*. They are alike in their belief that royalty and the ruling class are gods on earth and that all should cede to them, but in matters of sentiment they present quite different attitudes. Being satisfied with physical possession, Théophile's king will apply any force necessary to win Thisbé, whereas Gondebaut would prefer to gain Chryséide's love by kindness. He realizes that in matters of love the use of force ultimately proves futile. Although Théophile's characters undoubtedly deliver better poetry, those created by Mairet appear more human, more greatly endowed with sentiment, and as a result are more credible dramatic figures.

The opening of act III finds Bellaris and the two women free from prison and in search of an inn for a night's rest. The short scene with the unwilling innkeeper provides a comic touch in keeping with the mixture of genres. In the second scene Arimand, after a short lyric monologue inspired by Racan's *les Bergeries*, learns from Bellaris of Chryséide's escape. It is during this scene that Mairet includes an important exchange between hero and servant. In *l'Astrée* Bellaris, in order to facilitate Arimant's escape, suggests that they exchange clothes. Although Arimant hesitates to leave his faithful friend in prison, he is easily persuaded of the necessity of the move. Mairet develops this hesitation into a short-lived but true psychological dilemma in Arimand's soul. Caught between love of his mistress and duty to his servant, he struggles not knowing whether he should commit a cowardly act by abandoning Bellaris in such straits or a cruel act by remaining in prison and not seeking to ease Chryséide's torment. Love finally rules over him, and he agrees to the ploy. Indicative both of Mairet's understanding of the dramatic utility of such dilemmas and of his power of insight and analysis, this short scene is among the very first to signal the element which would transform theater—the dilemma-crisis to be found later at the heart of French classical tragedy.

Clearly realizing the attraction of the necessary scene between Chryséide and Arimand, Mairet increased the suspense of the moment by withholding it from the audience until act IV, scene 2. The lovers are finally joined and celebrate in their habitual lyric fashion the passage from misfortune to freedom and happiness. As Bellaris enters announcing the imminent arrival of the king and his troops, the couple submits again to fate as Arimand and his servant hurriedly escape.

The fifth act, dramatizing the final reunion of the lovers and their pardon by the king, follows the plot line of *l'Astrée* more closely than any preceding act. Mairet develops both the king's role and the importance of religion in the denouement. The king exists in the play to oppose Chryséide and Arimand. He is the obstacle personified. The king's role parallels that of the gods. Throughout the play he acts against the lovers, just as they believe the gods are working against them. Metaphorically it appears to be fate and the heavens causing their ills, factually it is the king. Arimand is held prisoner because of a war waged by the king, whose passion is the reason for Chryséide's imprisonment.

At the beginning of the king's first scene he reveals his basic belief in the relationship between gods and kings, speaking of "we kings who are half-gods" (II. 2. 574). Being half a god does not satisfy the king, however, and he looks forward to the time when his pleasures will make both gods and men envious. A change in attitude takes place in act IV, scene 1, when the king learns that Chryséide has escaped. His reaction to this event is the same as that of the hero to his misfortune. He believes mere man incapable of such a deed. The act must be the result of

First Attempts and First Success

superhuman power. He attacks the powers above him as the only objects worthy of his anger and declares himself their equal. His next move is to debase the gods, calling them creatures of man's invention and feared only by "le vulgaire." Finally he decides that they are mere idols, powerless gods made of iron and marble, and not worthy of his rage.

The conclusion of the play presents the resolution of the conflict between the king and the gods. Confronted by the *Sacrificateur*, the gods' representative on earth, the king feigns complete piety. When Chryséide says that to marry him would be a crime because she has promised herself to another, he replies, "Kings as well as Gods make all things permissible" (V. 3. 1532). Finally, when the heroine attempts to take asylum at the *Tombeau*, a holy place, the king decides to force her out despite the protests of the *Sacrificateur*. Before he can accomplish this, Arimand and Bellaris come on the scene demanding that Chryséide be set free. Because the king has promised to grant any wish to whomever brings in the person who helped her escape, the two friends each admit guilt.

This situation creates a dilemma in the mind of the king. Does he give in to violence and abduct Chryséide against the remonstrances of the *Sacrificateur*, or does he accede to the wishes of the others and unite the two lovers? He says, "No, I see that the Gods oppose my wishes. Heaven in revolt forbids my desire" (V. 3. 1665–66). Heaven forces the king to accept its will, and he acts following heaven's commands. He pardons the lovers, and at long last they are united. Heaven acted within the king, providing a solution to his dilemma and a conclusion to the play. Finally the king says to himself, "I believe that such diverse events all have their invisible source in Heaven" (V. 3. 1675–76). The king reaches the realization that all men must accept, that of the dependence of men, even kings, on the gods. From an initial indication in *l'Astrée* that the king's change of heart is somehow due to heavenly intervention, Mairet creates a conflict between the king and the gods basic to his character. He measures his own power against that of the superior beings, hoping to surpass them and then degrading them in his frustration. Given both the repeated theme of the gods' power to direct earthly events and the king's position in relation to the gods, the ending is much less arbitrary than might be imagined. The king's sudden realization or conversion marks the culminating point of a major theme as exemplified in a major character, concluding with an expression of the play's moral lesson.

We have already mentioned the contrast between the nature of the servants' roles and those of their master and mistress. The dichotomy between the two couples is particularly indicative of the state of theater at the time of Mairet's first play. Bellaris and Clarinde perform the active roles, while those of the two lovers are more static, more lyrical, more defined by language. Neither of the servants delivers a monologue, whereas Chryséide has one and Arimand three. Language and action—the former being the essential element of the pure pastoral, the latter the prime characteristic of tragicomedy—lack unification in *Chryséide et Arimand* as they do throughout the theater of this early age. It is an improvement that both necessary elements exist in the same play, but in order to produce rewarding theater they should be present to some extent in the same character, preferably the main character on whom the audience's interest centers. In order to note this problem more clearly, let us examine Arimand as representative of a character based primarily in language, similar in this respect to Pyrame and earlier heroes, but one who undergoes an essential change at the end of the play.

At the beginning of the play Chryséide and Arimand are held in different prisons. The image of the prison presents the basic characteristic of their state of being throughout almost the entire play. Their existence is qualified as an imprisonment, and the play represents essentially their search for freedom. Physically imprisoned by walls and chains, figuratively imprisoned by love, the characters have only one freedom—the freedom to speak. Body and will are enslaved, but the voice is free.[14] For this reason the totality of the character's action is found in his language. More specifically, freedom of speech means almost exclusively the liberty to complain, for it is in lamentation that the character spends the majority of his time. *Souffrir et se plaindre* ("suffer and complain") could even be stated as the motto of the sufferer.

First Attempts and First Success

Existing in full consciousness of his own condition, the suffering character is totally lucid. Although he may refer to his situation as *folie*, this must be understood as a madness which sharpens the mind rather than dulling it. He can thus translate his attitudes into speech, explain and comment on his plight. Again, this illustrates the extreme importance of language for the character. In the only action permitted him, he exteriorizes his mental state by means of the voice, resulting in *plaintes*.

A primary characteristic of the sufferer-type is his complete lack of will power. The relationship between Arimand and Bellaris illustrates this point. Any action, even any suggestion or decision about changing their state of fortune, comes from Bellaris. The role of the servant must of necessity provide an active element, missing from the hero, if the pair is to find an end to their misfortunes. Arimand's lack of volition only contains him within the present situation, permitting no other activity than that which defines his being, his speech. He is a closed circle from which he cannot make an escape, for the only action found within it is the very action which creates the circle. By speaking he both defines his character and participates in the only activity allowed him. An obvious alternative to his existence would be death, and in his pessimism Arimand sees this as the only end to his condition. By rejecting all help which would alter his situation, he seems to be fighting, albeit passively, for a maintenance of the status quo. The problem of those acting in the character's behalf is to find some means of destroying this petrification. As the character exists as a closed world, some element within his own existence must be reached to destroy his imprisonment.

Common sense tells Bellaris that Arimand is mistaken to refuse his help. As a servant interested in his master's well-being, he refuses to leave him in his fixed existence. Scenes of decision-making, in which plans for an alternative course of existence are formulated, occur five times during the course of the play. In act I, scene 2, Arimand is in prison and his friend tries to persuade him that he should exercise his reason and find a means of escape. Since that plea falls on deaf ears, Bellaris himself suggests an escape plan, and it works. In act II, scene 1, it is Chryséide's turn to escape. Bellaris, who has made his way to her prison, and Clarinde devise the scheme. But in act III, scene 2, the soldiers have recaptured Arimand. Again the faithful servant invents a plan whereby his master can escape. In act IV the hero and heroine meet for a short time, but, as the king is hunting for them in the region, Bellaris convinces Arimand that they must leave. In act V, scene 1, Chryséide has been recaptured by the king who plans to marry her immediately. After hearing the news from Bellaris, Arimand inveighs against the gods, but he then decides to take matters into his own hands and save Chryséide whatever the cost. Bellaris follows in amazement as Arimand runs off.

Why has the change taken place and the hero suddenly broken out of his character? The reason lies in Bellaris's misunderstanding of Arimand. At the news that the king has taken Chryséide, Arimand faints. Bellaris begs him to show more constancy, to bear his sorrow more stoically. Here is Bellaris's first mistake. Arimand cannot suffer without expressing his sorrow. He responds that he likes his sorrow too much to be distracted from it. Next Bellaris asks him to look at the matter "without passion" (V. 1. 1349). Again he misunderstands Arimand's character, for the hero cannot exist without passion. Finally Bellaris reaches a conclusion: common sense tells him that everything—gods and men—is against them because of Arimand's love, and thus the only way for the two friends to escape their wrath is for Arimand to stop loving Chryséide. Bellaris advises him, "The quickest and most certain remedy is for you to still your flame, to forget it and to be silent" (1375–76).

The final insult proves too much for Arimand. He rebounds and attacks Bellaris as a traitor. The servant then asks his master what he has decided, and Arimand reaches his decision: "To try once more, resolved to die or to see her again" (1395–96). His friend has attacked the one liberty which Arimand still possesses, the freedom to speak. In asking him to deny that freedom, he has asked Arimand to deny everything—the pains he has suffered, the love which makes him suffer, indeed, his very existence. Therein lies the key to

First Attempts and First Success

breaking the enclosing circle—attacking the element which defines it, the character's voice. By doing so Bellaris has forced Arimand to a redefinition of his character, one which includes the will to act. In this character change, Mairet gives yet another indication of the path to be followed in future theatrical endeavors. The sufferer, too strongly linked to the pure pastoral, must be rejected in favor of a more active, modern hero.

Mairet's first play represents very well the state of French theater of 1625, while possessing important new elements which he and other authors will develop further at a later date. The essential though short-lived psychological dilemmas in Arimand and the king, the dramatization of events rather than their relation by messengers, use of preparation and suspense—all of these factors combine to lift Mairet's tragicomedy above the general level of the times. Equally as important as these considerations is Mairet's realization of audience interest in an episode from the most popular literary product of that part of the century, and his ability to transform it into a dramatic work. Hardly a perfect dramatic creation, *Chryséide et Arimand* is noteworthy as the first work of a young man who will prove himself the leading dramatic author of this transitional period.

III Sylvie

Critics have been unable to agree on a definition or even a description of the genre of *Sylvie*, Mairet's second play.[15] For one critic it is primarily a pastoral with a few elements of tragicomedy; for another it is a *comédie de moeurs*. Yet another views the play as a chivalric romance set in the framework of the pastoral.[16] The author himself calls the play a pastoral tragicomedy, and the difficulty of definition lies precisely in that appellation. In an age when literary boundaries were collapsing and once separated forms merging with one another, the task of establishing a limiting definition is rendered almost impossible. What was once an element of tragedy has become an integral part of tragicomedy. Characteristic traits of the pastoral are found in new dramatic forms far removed from the older genre. The pastoral tragicomedy became the confluence of all earlier forms. It rejected certain elements, for example the tragic ending, farcical comedy, and the need for violent action, while retaining others proper to its character and, especially, necessary for pleasing its audience.

The play opens in the royal court of Candie where the prince Florestan, seeing a portrait, falls in love with the person represented. She is Méliphile, a Sicilian princess, and he vows to journey to Sicily and win her. In the second scene the audience learns of the play's major love interest. Sylvie, a shepherdess, loves and is loved by the prince Thélame. In a lyric monologue which totally lacks the exaggeration often found in pure pastorals, the heroine speaks of the innocent pleasures of love. She is soon joined by Philène, a shepherd, who suffers as a victim of unrequited love. The most celebrated scene of the play follows, the "Comédie ou Dialogue de Philène et de Sylvie," a set piece written in couplets in which the unhappy shepherd complains of the indifference of Sylvie, and she responds that he must renounce his attempts to change her attitude. After she runs off, Philène bemoans such treatment in a monologue of self-pity and lamentation. The fourth scene introduces us to the princely hero, Thélame, as his sister, Méliphile, questions him on his disguise as a shepherd. He admits to disguising himself in order to meet more freely with the person he loves. Learning that the object of the prince's affection is a shepherdess, Méliphile protests at such difference in social class, thus presenting the principal objection to the lovers' union. In the final scene of the act Sylvie and Thélame meet and speak of their love for each other.

The story of the second act concerns Sylvie and her family, more properly their plans to marry her as they see fit. Having learned of Thélame's visits to their daughter, and fearing the prince can have no other motive than to abuse her innocence and deceive her, the parents want her to marry Philène. As a shepherd, her father says, he should have a shepherd as a son-in-law. Furthermore, despite the mother's objections, Sylvie's father will force her to bend to his will. The second conflict thereby enters the picture, parental authority. Making no mention of the prince, Sylvie protests that she is too young to marry and wants to dedicate herself to Diana, the virgin goddess.

First Attempts and First Success

Realizing that he cannot win Sylvie's love by any other means, Philène in act III has recourse to ruse. He persuades Dorise, who loves him as he loves Sylvie, to pretend that she has a gnat in her eye just as Thélame passes by and to implore his help. As the prince leans toward her trying to blow the gnat from Dorise's eye, Sylvie and Philène are strategically located, so that Sylvie believes Thélame is kissing the other girl and betraying her. The two lovers meet shortly afterward, and Sylvie bitterly accuses the prince of fooling her with his beautiful words of empty artifice. Philène's scheme might have worked, had not Dorise recounted her interesting adventure to Sylvie at the end of the act, thereby destroying the illusion and restoring the original situation. The ruse succeeds only in creating a passing conflict which evaporates once the truth becomes known.

Act IV serves as a counterpart to act II in that it presents the parental conflict from Thélame's side. His father, the king, has decided to have him marry a princess from Cyprus in order to establish peace by bringing the two kingdoms closer together. Although his counselor advises patience in ending the prince's liaison with the shepherdess, the king believes violence to be the only means possible. He fears that her ambition could be harmful to the state. The second scene shows Sylvie and Thélame discussing the possibility of such an attitude on the part of the king. Thélame states categorically that he will not give up Sylvie nor do anything else for the good of the state that would destroy his own happiness. As he presses Sylvie to gather her pleasures while she is young, she responds by telling him the story of a shepherdess who killed herself as a result of abandoning her honor. Soon after Thélame leaves, the court guards enter and on the king's order escort Sylvie to the palace.

At the beginning of the final act Florestan, the prince from the play's first scene, is found by Dorise and Philène as he is lying at the edge of the forest. He learns from them that he is in Sicily, and also hears of the means by which he can win Méliphile. Sylvie and Thélame have been placed under a magic spell from which they wake periodically, each one believing the other dead. The situation has lasted for over a week, and despite the king's desires to have it ended no means can be found. Only a knight endowed with great courage can break the spell, and by doing so he will earn the right to claim Méliphile as his bride. The scene shifts to the palace where the effects of the unfortunate spell are seen. The two lovers awake in turn, discovering the other dead at their side, and each laments the others death in passionate, tragic terms. Aided by the advice of a heavenly voice, Florestan finally succeeds in breaking the charm by fighting through phantoms and black monsters. The voice then instructs the king to accept Sylvie as his daughter-in-law as a just reward for her fidelity. It is the will of the gods that she be crowned. The king accepts heaven's edict; he also joins Florestan to Méliphile, and Philène accepts Dorise to conclude the play happily.

In the composition of the play Mairet shows the influence of two major sources, two plays that we have already mentioned as essential to the early development of the author's talent—Théophile's *Pyrame et Thisbé* and Racan's *Bergeries*.[17] *Sylvie* represents the next logical step after the two earlier works and results, as it were, of their natural marriage, truly creating the French pastoral tragicomedy. In this, *Sylvie* marks an important date in the history of French theater. One of the first, if not the very first author to combine the pastoral with the tragicomedy, Mairet began a vogue which continued into the 1630s. Although some scenes are in direct imitation of Racan or Théophile, and although many of the situations represented were commonplace in pastoral or tragicomedy, Mairet sufficiently modified the tone and character of both genres to give the play a unified character. The pastoral eases its rigidity and loses its exclusively lyric qualities, becoming less monotonous and more humanized. The tragicomedy rids itself of unnecessary and encumbering details. The result is a freer, easier, and more harmonious whole, whose simplicity and clarity are in sharp contrast to the tone of earlier dramatic works. In modifying both the emotional tone and the structure of the genres, Mairet helped prepare the dramatic movement of the 1630s.

The genre to which Mairet owes the greatest debt in *Sylvie* is the pastoral.[18] Specific changes which the author brought to

First Attempts and First Success

the genre will show his further progress in creating drama for stage presentation and audience interest.[19] As a dramatic form the pastoral suffered from an overabundance of artificial situations and conventions. Mairet eliminates important ones, for example, the oracle, the satyr, and the magician. He limits the use of magic to one act without destroying the essentially natural unity of the play. On a more human level, the one instance of ruse fails, though the priest proposes the moral that such innocent illusions are permitted in matters of love. Of the pastoral conventions retained, many are weakened by the author and remain merely as vestiges of the older genre. For example, the pastoral element of disguise is present, but of no dramatic consequence. Thélame's dress as a shepherd fools no one; all know he is the prince.

The characters in the pastoral often lacked sufficient variety and depth to save them from the monotonous rigidity of conventionality which hampered the genre in the eyes of the public. Realizing the importance of fully developed characters for successful drama, Mairet creates roles in *Sylvie* which are believable and at times striking in their realism. Fundamental to this important progress is Mairet's better understanding of the role of language in theater. Rather than functioning as an end in itself, language must be integrated with the characters' actions and become an extension of their roles. No single character performs, as did Chryséide and Arimand, as disembodied language. Escaping the single dimensional quality of the earlier hero and heroine, the characters in *Sylvie* gain in depth and believability.

Sylvie and her parents are not disguised aristocrats, but true country people. Breaking a long-standing artificiality Mairet does not have the heroine revealed at the end of the play as a lost royal princess. She remains a sherpherdess, true to her original identity. Even the conventional role of the sufferer is modified. Philène is in the same line of characters as Pyrame and Arimand, those who spend the majority of their time complaining. Once he realizes that he will gain nothing by his complaints, however, he does not hesitate to go into action, breaking the normal pattern as seen in Arimand. Dramatic preparation is also evident in Philène's role. Rather than have his agreement to marry Dorise at the end of the play a surprising new element, the author has prepared for it by having him promise earlier to respond to her love, once he knows definitely that Sylvie will not love him. The heroine herself is a marvel of characterization. Fresh, lively, witty, totally devoid of conventionality, she shows the great progress made by Mairet, and theater, in creating believable characters on stage.

A major difference between the basic nature of the pastoral and that of *Sylvie* can be seen in the mistrust of language which the characters express. After a charmingly lyrical, but essentially frivolous bit of conversation in which both hero and heroine compliment each other in terms of imagery common to the pastoral, Sylvie cuts Thélame's lyric flights short, expressing her impatience at such language and qualifying their preceding *badinage* as "foolish chatter." Defending himself in a later scene against Sylvie's suspicions of his betrayal, Thélame says that he is not "among those who give mere language as proof of their affection" (IV. 3. 1433–34). He is not, he says, a courtesan whose love consists only of flattering words. Words spoken are never entirely believed. They must be supported by action. The passage from the pastoral ethic of language to the newer ethic of action is evident in the characters' attitude. Although they spend most of their time in speaking, they realize the incomplete and illusory quality of words.

The two sources of conflict in the play complement and reinforce each other, as the young people's actions counter the accepted parent-child relationship as well as the accepted mode of conduct as determined by the social structure. Indeed, the necessity of enforcing parental authority on apparently rebellious children grows from the parents' social awareness. Sylvie's parents object to Thélame because he is of a higher social class. In order to remedy the situation they will choose a proper husband for her, exercising their parental rights and duties. Animated by similar sentiments, the king decides his son must marry a princess, not only for reasons of the state's well-being, but also to keep a peasant from the throne. The two lovers are aware of these accepted beliefs, but only partially share the strict attitudes which divide them from their

First Attempts and First Success

parents. Creating no internal dilemma in hero or heroine, the conflict remains exterior, forced upon them by others and never an integral part of their character. Sylvie hesitates only slightly, Thélame not at all, at the thought of the social distance separating them and the parental authority forcing them apart. Though the obstacle lacks the unreality of Chryséide and Arimand's supposed persecution by the fates, it does not possess the inner psychological reality necessary for a true dilemma. That step has not yet been reached. The play is essentially hero and heroine against those in authority.

In *Sylvie* a person's age determines to a great extent his character, actions, and dramatic utility, as well as his relationship to the other characters. The two groups are polarized—the old people believe that parental authority permits full control over the young, whereas the young people chafe under what they consider oppression. It is a conflict, conventional in the theater of the time, "of two beings, one representing a respectable code of honorable conduct and the other the spontaneity of the heart."[20] The young people are animated by love and freedom, whereas the old people act against this freedom and thus directly against the love of the young.

Innocence with its implicit freedom is that quality of existence which most properly defines youth; and loss of innocence, more a state of mind than a purely physical trait, defines the passage from youth to old age. The generations are separated by conflict in character, attitudes, and actions, but most basically they are polarized as they represent two manners of life. Those of the younger generation struggle to preserve their innocence and freedom, thus to preserve their youth itself, while the other people attempt to impose their own desires on the children, forcing them into their own condition of existence and bringing about a loss of youth. The specific issue is forced marriage, contracted by the parents and combatted by the children.

In the old people's eyes, the wishes and desires of the children should coincide with those of their parents, or rather the young should have no desires, so that their parents' will may entirely dictate their own. This is *le droit de la naissance*. Damon says to his wife that their daughter's "wishes depend upon ours and will be commanded by them" (II. 2. 715–16). His attitude is unswerving. Mairet, however, slightly mitigates this position by giving Sylvie's mother a modified opinion. Although she agrees in principle with Damon, she feels that since the matter directly concerns Sylvie, the girl should be consulted. Damon quickly puts an end to such a suggestion.

In face of such opposition the children display a singular attitude. They neither openly admit their love, nor do they attempt to defy the parents and consciously provoke a break. Sylvie asks that she never marry, but devote herself to worship of Diana. Thélame merely asks to spend one or two more years in the pleasures permitted to young people. Their attitude is simply that they want to continue to pursue the life of youth. Rather than consciously rejecting the responsibilities of age, they seem to be attempting to preserve the liberty in which their youth functions, and forced marriage represents for them the destruction of that freedom. While the old people have filial obligation and recourse to power on their side, the young appear powerless in the conflict. Indeed, their only weapon is their youth itself, which they consequently present as justification for their attitudes and actions. The old people reject this, calling it merely an excuse, and believe that the young people are acting in rebellion.

Parallel to the conflict caused by parental control is the obstacle which grows from the social context in which the characters live and act. This social structure performs, however, a different function within the characters than the youth–old age dichotomy. Whereas a person's age largely determined his attitudes, no such determination results from his social position. Rather than having differing attitudes according to their rank in the social stratification, the characters all reflect the same attitude, created by the very existence of the social order. They are conditioned to react in a certain manner whenever any change takes place in the order, more specifically whenever anyone transgresses its bounds. To break from one's social group in an attempt to join with an individual from another represents a crime. This is the cause of conflict and consequent action in the plays. Almost all characters hold the opinion that the social structure must remain unbroken, and that all members must stay within the group into which they were born. One finds,

First Attempts and First Success

therefore, strong defense of the existing system, of its authority, and a rejection of those who do not conform to it. The social groups are understood to be distinct, but dramatically the author scarcely differentiates between them. Members of both classes show similar attitudes and comport themselves in much the same manner. Economic conditions neither divide them nor enter into discussion. The two classes are simply royalty and subjects. Most importantly, both classes are extremely conscious of their position and careful to remain within its bounds. Furthermore, they are anxious to keep other members within it.

The problem in *Sylvie* arises precisely because one member from each group, though implicitly accepting the division, has broken ranks and joined in love with someone from the other group, specifically Thélame, a prince, and Sylvie, a shepherdess. Their concern, as evidenced in the discussion of youth versus old age, is the freedom to love whom they choose. No other character in the play accepts this freedom. Indeed all combat it overtly. When Thélame confesses to his sister that he is in love, she immediately responds that she hopes the object of his affection is worthy of his love and his social equal. Her questioning stems from an acute consciousness of their position as royalty, understood as a social stratum rather than as a ruling class in a political sense. The key words are "rank" and "blood." The prince's mistress and eventual mate must equal him in social rank, or else his choice is wrong and must be combatted by those within his class. Only social standing which equals his own can make her worthy to receive his fortune and share the throne with him, in other words, to enter into his social order. Sylvie is not of the proper standing; therefore the prince's choice is unwise, and his father, the king, must prevent the affair from proceeding any further.

Knowing that the person one loves is of the same social class presents justification for pursuing that love. Upon seeing the portrait of a beautiful woman, prince Florestan asks "son nom et sa naissance" (her name and her birth, I. 1. 40). As the answer comes that she is a princess, he breathes a sigh of relief, knowing that he may love only a person of such high standing. Were she not of royal birth, he could neither love her nor hope to obtain her, as his honor would forbid it.

Remaining in one's own class stands as a matter of honor to oneself and also to the class collectively.

The lower class shows the same concern about not straying from the group and its authority. Damon wishes his daughter to marry Philène, a shepherd. His reasoning lies in his social consciousness. Although he knows that his daughter is in love with a prince, such an alliance is simply impossible. Believing that the prince may persuade his daughter to relinquish her honor, Damon moves quickly and purposefully toward his daughter's marriage with the shepherd. His attitude, even his reasoning and vocabulary, parallel Méliphile's reaction to the news that her brother loves a shepherdess. Considering the prince's most likely motives, Damon says: "I think this Lord would only lower himself to see her in order to pass his time and deceive her" (II. 1. 539-40). This echoes Méliphile's conviction that such a love could only be feigned, or at most a passing fancy. For that reason the prince's intentions toward Sylvie are immediately suspicious. That he should seek love from someone below him, i.e., that he should leave his own class, is dishonorable, according to Damon. A mistrust arises, not of the upper class as a whole, but rather of anyone who goes beyond the bounds of his class.

Mairet thus uses his characters' social consciousness as a motive for action in two possible ways. If the loved one is of the same social condition, the lover moves to accomplish their union. If lovers are not of the same condition, the other members of society combat their union in order to protect the existing social order.

The desire to keep characters from leaving their own group is a family matter as well as a social matter, for the main characters in *Sylvie* are two families, as well as representing two classes. They use family authority in addition to societal pressure to contain the hopeful lovers, and the author thus joins the two areas of conflict. The underlying motive is the preservation of honor, in this case family honor. The means of guarding it lie in the parents' power over their children and the children's duty of filial obligation. Family pressure provided the first cause of the flight of Chryséide and Arimand. In that play, however, Mairet did not exploit the issue further, and he

First Attempts and First Success

did not even show the parents as active partners in the play. In *Sylvie* he uses the parents' desire to decide their child's future as a means of providing action, linking it closely to the previously discussed social consciousness.

The reactions of Sylvie's parents arise from the fear that her conduct will stain their family honor. Their first words introduce this idea. Overhearing her husband mutter something about unreasonable desires, Sylvie's mother immediately assumes that "our daughter has sullied her honor" (II. 1. 524). Their daughter's honor means simply her chastity. Being even more explicit, Damon says that the prince's desire is to attack her innocence and thus to shame the poor family. The link between the daughter's "honor" and the family honor is extremely close. Once she has heard Damon's reasons for suspecting their daughter, Macée's attitude changes. She does not share her husband's damning opinion of the prince's desires or his innate mistrust of the prince. She says that he is too good to abuse their daughter. Lest this appear a simplistic opinion, Mairet also shows Macée's concern with honor. She believes that the prince himself could not attempt such dishonorable acts, as he also values honor. Her opinions cause great consternation in Damon, and he upbraids her for supporting Sylvie and for seeming unconcerned with the family's honor.

The king also gives great thought to the problem of family repute, although his concept of honor is more far-reaching than that of the shepherd parents. The prince, he says, is caught in a bond which tarnishes the splendor of the Sicilian name. Not only does Thélame harm the family honor, but also the honor of the kingdom over which the family rules. As to the ultimate consequences of his dishonoring act, the king appears as concerned with himself as he is with his son: "I have to fear for my shame" (IV. 1. 1346).

An important element of the conclusion of *Sylvie* is the resolution of the social difference between the two lovers. It takes place after the spell has been broken. The Voice speaks, instructing the king according to the will of the gods: "Raise the baseness and the inequality of her social standing by her faithfulness, and honor her virtue with a crown. This is the will of the gods and their commandment" (V. 3. 2163–66). The social barrier ceases to exist, having been eliminated by the will of heaven. The resolution thus arises from the religious structure as it works providentially to bring about its desires.

The problem of defining the genre of *Sylvie* proves ultimately an unnecessary task. The preceding areas of conflict, for example, belong equally to the pastoral and to the tragicomedy of the period. The use of magic shows the author's desire to please an avid public, as well as giving evidence of his debt to earlier dramatic forms. In molding the diverse influences which led up to the writing of *Sylvie*—portrayal of purified sentiments more commonly found in the novel than in theater, chivalric exploits from the tragicomedy or the novel, plot details and situations previously seen in pastoral and in tragicomedy, emotional tone and temperament influenced by Théophile and Racan—Mairet was forced to find, or rather to create, a dramatic form in which all could exist in a harmonious whole. The only name which can be given to that form is the one Mairet himself chose—*la tragi-comédie pastorale*.

CHAPTER 3

Mairet and Progress of the Unities

I *Quarrel of the Unities*

BEGINNING his career in 1625, Mairet could rightly say that he did not know of the existence of the unities. The rules governing the time that the dramatic work could represent, restricting its spatial representation, and limiting it to one main action with possible secondary interests were generally unknown to the authors before 1628. Indeed, the greatest flurry of discussions about the rules and conflicting dramatic theories did not begin until 1630.[1] Before that time, the predominant dramatic forms were the various permutations of the pastoral and the tragicomedy. They were the irregular genres, influenced both by the Latin *drame libre* and by the simple necessity of responding to the public's desire for exciting, varied spectacles. Rich in action, the works of the early part of the century satisfied that public need.

There existed however a third group, neither dramatic poets nor avid spectators, which was concerned with theater. The *doctes*, the scholars, among whom the most prominent was Chapelain,[2] were aware at a much earlier date of the rules of dramatic composition. Through their studies of sixteenth century Italian theoreticians they learned of the unities, as well as the ancient Greek and Roman authors, and became converted to the belief that the application of certain rules was indispensable for the creation of a literary work. The ensuing discussions and debates centered thus not solely on the application or nonapplication of the unities, but also on the mentality expressed in the conviction of the doctrine's absoluteness. Although in general those who argued for observance of the unities, called the regulars, were also partisans of the belief in their utter necessity for poetic success, the two issues must be understood as separate.

The distinction will prove essential to a proper comprehension of Mairet's position. Examination of three documents will illustrate the diverging points of view and permit an understanding of the poet's thoughts and his role in the debates.

In 1628 Jean de Schelandre published his tragicomedy *Tyr et Sidon,* a reworking of a tragedy he had written twenty years earlier. The work was preceded by a preface written by François Ogier, which has come to be regarded as an apologia for the irregular genres, those which did not comply with the rule regarding unity of time. Apart from various criticisms of the overdependence on messengers, sudden recognitions, and fortunate chance encounters in the plays of the ancients, Ogier's remarks contain three major points. Attacking first the respect which the scholars felt was due the ancients, Ogier says that tastes vary and change with the times, and that different nations react in varying manners to similar problems. Imitation of the older authors, he argues, should not be slavish copying of their precepts, but should function according to "the proper character (*génie*) of our country according to the tastes of our language."[3] He is pleading for poetic invention based not on simple adoption of previously existing principles, but on the adaptation of those principles, meaning the unities, to the writer's own situation. Supporting his argument for necessary change, he claims that the ancients themselves did not always bend to the rules, following their public's wishes rather than a set of arbitrary precepts. Ogier obviously felt that in their limitation of dramatic possibilities the unities ran against the desires of the contemporary public. The spectator, and not the scholar, should dictate the tenor of dramatic creation. This belief underlies the arguments of all the irregulars, as they reacted against the restrictions of the rules, which would inevitably result, they believed, in a loss of public interest in theater.

Ogier's primary argument centers likewise on concern for audience reaction. He criticizes the ancients for basing their dramas on talk rather than action. "Poetry, and especially that composed for the theater, is created only for pleasure and diversion, and this pleasure can result only from the variety of events which are represented."[4] The goal of the theatrical arts is pleasure; that pleasure is accomplished by variety and action. This was the reigning aesthetic for drama in the early years of the century and even into the 1630s. The major characteristic was freedom from restricting rules. Alexandre Hardy's theater typifies the conception of drama as action whose purpose is to captivate and entertain the public. Violence of expression and emotion, numerous incidents included simply for the sake of action, dependence of events on external circumstances—such were the traits of plays written by authors who subscribed to the aesthetic of freedom. As a reaction to the static sixteenth-century tragedy, the move toward theatrical representation of action was laudatory, in that it did much to broaden interest in drama and win theater its audience.

In his 1630 preface to *La Généreuse Allemande, deuxième journée,* André Mareschal repeated Ogier's major points. "The goal of this sort of (dramatic) poem is entirely to present action, and that of the action is to please."[5] Any rule limiting the poet's dramatic options, resulting in a reduction of action, would automatically result in a lessening of pleasure and a decline in audience interest. The company of the Hôtel de Bourgogne was especially concerned about the latter matter. The established theater reacted unfavorably to plays written according to the unities. Its public derived great visual pleasure from the multiple decors used by the company, and Bellerose was loath to renounce such a popular device in favor of mere representation of a single place.

The most heated discussion concerned the unity of time, called the twenty-four-hour rule. The irregulars stated that the ancients did not always submit to it, and that when they did the result was an unreal telescoping of events in order to restrict them to the alloted time span. Chapelain's response, dated November 29, 1630, to Antoine Godeau's questioning about the necessity of the rule is an essential document in understanding the progress, or perhaps lack of progress, of the unities in the eyes of the dramatic poets. It is the famous "Lettre sur la règle des vingt-quatre heures"[6] and argues the point of view opposed to the total freedom defended by such authors as Ogier and Mareschal.

Unfortunately Godeau's initial letter to Chapelain has been lost, but it would seem to present arguments similar to those of

Ogier, for Chapelain's response reads like a point by point rebuttal of the earlier preface. He flatly denies Ogier's principal contentions—that the object of dramatic poetry is pleasure, and that the goal is reached by inclusion of great variety of actions. Likewise he belittles credence in the omnipotence of the theatrical public by stating that the poet should accommodate himself to his public's desires (*inclination*), but not to its vices. Clearly Chapelain's view of the relationship of dramatic poet to public differs markedly from that expressed by the earlier writer.

The aesthetics expressed by the two men vary to the same degree. The partisans of the "irregular" school based their art on pure invention, while Chapelain argued for dramatic creation founded on imitation. In his own words, "imitation alone makes all poetry."[7] The goal of the dramatic poem, according to Chapelain, was not to please the audience, but to move its soul, to purge its passions. The means of accomplishing this end was imitation of truth, an imitation "so perfect that there appears no difference between that which is imitated and that which imitates,"[8] in other words between reality and the work of art. The audience was to believe itself present at a veritable event. The key word for Chapelain was verisimilitude (*vraisemblance*). Therein lay the crux of the argument and the great criterion of judgment. The dramatic poem must above all be believable; the means toward that end is perfect imitation. Furthermore, if pleasure is to be sought in theater, it should proceed from order and *vraisemblance*.

Arguing from the basis of verisimilitude Chapelain presents the case for two of the three unities—unity of action and unity of time. The eye can only properly take in one action, otherwise it gets lost in the ensuing *embarras*. It is not reasonable to assume that the spectator can either follow or believe the tortuous complications of certain plots. Concentration is thus demanded, rather than rampant multiplicity of actions. Concerning the representation of time, Chapelain makes the same case, implying that the subject chosen by the author should permit proper accomplishment within the limited time period. Otherwise his work would sin against the accepted goal—the imitation of a totally credible action presented in dramatic form.

In order to bear fruit Chapelain's theories could not remain the sole domain of the *doctes*. Presenting his beliefs in a literary discussion he would have been speaking in a void, were there no means of lifting them to the realm of poetic practice. The case of the regulars had been clearly stated; it remained to apply their opinions to dramatic composition, and in doing so to present them before the theatrical public. That task would belong to Mairet.

In his preface to *Silvanire*, published in 1631 and entitled "Préface en forme de discours poétique,"[9] Mairet explains the genesis of the work. The comte de Carmail and the cardinal de la Valette had suggested around 1628-29 that he look to the Italian dramatic pastoral and compose a work with all the rigors found in that genre. Believing that French dramatic compositions did not equal the beauties of the Italian, the literary-minded gentlemen were anxious that Mairet find the source of the beauty and apply it to his next play. Their underlying desire was to elevate contemporary drama from the depths of artistic chaos in which they believed it was foundering. Mairet discovered that the secret of the Italians was simply that they modeled their works on the ancient Greeks and Latins, in other words they followed the classical unities more religiously than did the French. It is indeed possible, if not probable, that Carmail and la Valette had told him precisely that.

The preface itself may stand at least in part as an *Ars Poetica* of the moment. The theories Mairet proposes concerning the theatrical genres and the unities are not of his own invention, but are rather representative of the state of dramatic theory at that time as seen by the partisans of the rules. The sections not dealing specifically with the limitations are of even more general application. Examination of them may serve to clarify the authors' own comprehension of their art and their role during this transitional period.

Tragedy, according to Mairet, was the representation of a distressful heroic adventure; it was the mirror of the fragility of human affairs. The subject of the tragedy had to be well known and drawn from history. Its style was elevated in order to express the acts and passions of people of high quality. The dramatic action begins in glory and magnificence, only to end in misery. Comedy, on the other hand, was to begin in turbulence, ending joyously. The comic play portrayed private adventures with no danger to life. The style, in keeping with the more common people portrayed (Mairet uses the term "médiocre"), was simple. The subject was imagined but nonetheless believable. Tragicomedy partook of the essence of both genres, while the pastoral belonged properly with comedy.

Mairet speaks of only two unities, making no mention of the unity of place. Concerning the unity of action he states that a play should have "une maîtresse et principale action" and that other interests or actions in the play should have a definite relationship to it, like the lines from the circumference to the center of the circle. The greatest debates, however, took place over the unity of time. It was to this rule that the irregulars objected most violently. Mairet states that it is one of the fundamental laws of theater. In agreement with Chapelain's earlier statements, he expresses the opinion that the basis of pleasure in the theater is verisimilitude. Supporting that conception of theatrical pleasure he offers the following definition of drama: "an active and pathetic representation of things as though they were truly happening at the time, and whose principal end is the pleasure of the imagination."[10] The restraint of the time rule, as the ancients showed, was most conducive to the desired believability.

Aware of the problems which could arise from rigorous application of the unities, Mairet sympathizes with those authors who felt that their best effects were being summarily outlawed. There can result, he admits, a certain sterility or austerity in the dramatic action from the compression of the subject into a period of twenty-four hours. Mairet's preface is by no means a condemnation of those who did not follow the rules. Apart from rather adamantly stating that the pastoral must respect the unities, perhaps because *Silvanire* is a pastoral, Mairet simply says that those works that follow the rules of the ancients are more accomplished than those that do not. The preface is not a drum-beating, trumpet-sounding call to judgment, with Mairet the avenging angel dispatching the regulars to salvation and the irregulars to perdition. The author conceived it as a tract of general interest, a means of presenting certain dramatic concepts to the public. The way to win his audience was not to condemn as unworthy of attention the theatrical form from which they had derived pleasure for years. Mairet's role in the theoretical discussions was primarily that of a popularizer. Closer to the public than were the scholars, he functioned as an intermediary, interpreting and explaining the classical unities in easily comprehensible terms.

This relatively undogmatic attitude toward necessary application of the rules does not mask deeper convictions on Mairet's part. He himself, despite his pronouncements, was not convinced of the absoluteness of the doctrine or, for that matter, of any doctrine. The section of the preface to *Silvanire* dealing with the poet illustrates Mairet's separation from such pure theoreticians as Chapelain. In it he distinguishes between two distinct sets of characteristics necessary to the true poet. The first are "natural qualities," including the capacity of imagination and invention, fired by a powerful inclination to poetry. The poet must feel himself pushed by the "divine fury," the enthusiasm which can only be called poetic genius. Mairet uses the term "Nature" to categorize these qualities. The "foreign qualities" fall more easily under the title "Art"—the art of making verses, learned through study and supported by a knowledge of one's language, philosophy, the humanities, etc. Nature and Art are both essential to poetic creation, according to the poet, but the *sine qua non* is Nature, without which Art can accomplish nothing. The virtues of a good poet are to a great extent endowed qualities rather than learned. The weakness of pure doctrine is admitted. One is born a poet.

This attitude would explain, for example, how Mairet could write the highly irregular comedy *Les Galanteries du duc d'Ossonne* after composing the regular *Silvanire*. He did not consider the rules absolutes. They were to be applied when the subject of the dramatic poem permitted them, and could be conveniently ignored if the author's poetic genius dictated it. Throughout his career Mairet laid great importance on invention. He was most pleased with those works which were of his own creation, rather than adaptations of already existing works. His greatest strength as a dramatist, he felt, was precisely the capacity for imagination and invention. Obviously he hoped to be known as an author who created and wrote great plays, rather than as one who doggedly followed a set of rules, no matter how accomplished. Mairet's resolution in writing *Silvanire* was to present a work which followed the classical unities as did the Italian pastorals. Acknowledging the force of the rules and arguing in the preface for their general acceptance, Mairet nonetheless shows himself to be less the total partisan of the regulars than may be assumed.

II Silvanire

More so than his other plays, Mairet's *Silvanire*,[11] a pastoral tragicomedy staged in 1629–30, was a play done on command. Suggested to the author by men on whom he depended for both support and sustenance, the play was undertaken initially to please them. *Silvanire* does not stand as a work of inspiration but as one of circumstance, typifying the close, at times intimate, relationship between the author, the written work, and the protectors. This was simply one of the facts of the author's artistic and personal life. Written also with a particular purpose in mind, exemplification of the Italian unities in a French dramatic work, the play has a didactic basis. This framework provides the major historic and literary interest of the play. But both reasons—personal and didactic—help to explain Mairet's initial choice in the writing of *Silvanire*, the decision to adapt an already existing work rather than to write one of pure invention.

Mairet based his play on d'Urfé's *Sylvanire*,[12] a 1625 dramatization of an episode from *l'Astrée*. Since d'Urfé's pastoral imitated Italian dramatic form, an immediate resemblance appears between the earlier writer's completed work and the one projected by Mairet. The selection of *Sylvanire* as a subject for Mairet's adaptation resulted most likely from a combination of various decisions, strengthened by the author's innate dramatic sense—the original suggestion that he write a work in the vein of the Italians; the earlier success of *Chryséide et Arimand*, his previous adaptation of an episode taken from *l'Astrée*; continued public interest in d'Urfé's novel and in dramatic adaptations of it; Mairet's great success with *Sylvie*, also a pastoral tragicomedy; and finally, an understanding of the ease with which the

Mairet and Progress of the Unities

genre would fit into the context of the unities. Mairet was not so concerned with the creation of a new drama in *Silvanire* as he was with writing a play as an example of a particular form.

The dramatic action is preceded by a prologue spoken by "Honest Love." He justifies his often criticized conduct, explaining that he never causes illegitimate passion, only virtuous emotion. Though his doings may begin in difficulty, they always achieve a happy ending. In this manner the prologue also describes the action of *Silvanire* and of comedy as understood by Mairet. Act I begins with a discussion between Aglante, the play's hero, and Hylas about the proper way to love. A commonplace in the pastoral and those literary forms influenced by it, the scene contrasts Aglante's constancy with Hylas's desire to love any and all who would love him. Learning that Silvanire's parents intended to have her marry Théante, a rich shepherd, Aglante admits in his distress that she is the one whom he loves. In five years' time she has done nothing to return his love, he confides to his friend. Silvanire herself enters the scene shortly thereafter, and her disdain of Aglante seems to give credence to his fears. In a monologue opening act II Silvanire admits that she does love the unfortunate hero, but that duty to her parents forbids her to tell him so. Since he is poor, her parents would never consent to their union. The heroine is soon joined by Tirinte, another shepherd, who declares his love for her. She tells him of a dream which, she fears, foretells great suffering for her. Silvanire also mentions the love of her friend Fossinde for Tirinte, hoping he will show interest in her rather than in the heroine, but Tirinte rejects any thought of Fossinde.

In a conversation in act III Silvanire, while still refusing to admit that she loves Aglante, explains to him why she will not return his love. Honor, she says, forces her to remain silent, to preserve her virtue. She states that she hates love and will withstand its onslaught. Although Hylas dismisses honor as an invention of old people who want to deprive youth of its pleasure, Silvanire will not be dissuaded from her stand. Up to this point the play is purely discussion—Aglante and Hylas on love, Silvanire and her parents on marriage, Hylas, Aglante, and Silvanire on honor. It is toward the end of the act that the event takes place which will precipitate the play's conclusion. Alciron, a friend of Tirinte, gives him a magic mirror which will persuade Silvanire to love him. The act ends as the heroine, looking into the mirror, is stunned by what she sees and swoons. The characters soon learn that she has fallen into a debilitating lethargy and is near the point of death. Tirinte, realizing the cause of her state, races off to find Alciron, and Aglante faints upon hearing the news. As Silvanire and her parents enter on their way to pray at a shrine for her recovery, she kisses Aglante, but soon falls deeper into her illness. In her one moment of wakefulness she admits her love for the hero, and asks that she and Aglante be united in marriage before her death. The parents consent.

The next morning, after Silvanire has supposedly died and been placed in her tomb, Tirinte learns from Alciron the secret of the mirror. Silvanire is not dead, but merely in a deep sleep from which a potion will wake her. They proceed to the tomb, awaken the heroine, and Tirinte ties to convince her that the strength of his love has brought her back to life. Unable to persuade her to flee with him, he tries to use force. Aglante arrives at the tomb interrupting the attempted crime, and Tirinte is led away to be judged by the Druids. Silvanire's father then decides to revoke his previous decision to allow the marriage of hero and heroine, and that parental injunction is also appealed to the Druids. In an ending befitting the comic order of the play, Silvanire and Aglante are allowed to marry, and Fossinde and Tirinte also agree to be wed. The play ends with several short purely lyric scenes in the pastoral vein. They are in the same mold as the chorus speeches which end each act with a moralistic lesson, speaking of love, the age of gold, innocence, honor and virtue, avarice, and other pastoral commonplaces.

The changes which Mairet made in d'Urfé's play have two general purposes. First, they lighten the action, eliminating certain characters and events, thereby allowing the play to fit more readily into the form dictated by the unities. Second, they give the characters more life, as their sentiments and reactions take on greater importance than the simple events. The author thus rejects the overabundance of action of the Italian drama that d'Urfé followed. Rather than an invention or an adaptation, the play may be considered a concentration, as it focuses on the essential aspects of the story. Numerous monologues that serve only to slow the dramatic action are dropped; the character of the satyr and the subplot he represents are eliminated; Adraste, who is madly in love with Silvanire and who provides some comic relief in d'Urfé's play, has no place in Mairet's. The love of Hylas for a shepherdess who never appears likewise is not mentioned in Mairet's play, making of inconstancy's defender the hero's confidant rather than a truly interested active party in the play's intrigue. The author reduces the action to the love of Silvanire and Aglante, her parents' refusal to consent, and Tirinte's attempt to win the heroine for himself. The simplified action can proceed more quickly and more surely than did d'Urfé's often langorous pacing of the drama, slowed even more by numerous unnecessary repetitions.

Mairet's additions are of minor importance; for example, Silvanire's dream (II, 2) is a convenient yet common way of exciting suspense. An essential change in the verse form must be noted. D'Urfé had imitated the Italians even to their verse, an irregular poetic line, which in the French play became a curious sort of free verse. Mairet rejected this form, choosing instead to use the French alexandrine.

In general the characters of d'Urfé's play are less fully developed than those of Mairet's *Silvanire*, more static and therefore less dramatic. Remaining on an almost didactic level, they never truly converse but present opposing points of view as in a formalized debate. They never succeed in escaping from the imprisonment of their own lines and in becoming believable characters. Mairet's major improvement lies in this particular area. The heroine provides a good example. Because of her harsh, often bitter lines and a lack of modulation in the character, Sylvanire, d'Urfé's heroine, appears haughty, almost mockingly vicious in her initial scene with Aglante. Mairet's heroine is tempered, more believable because she does not attack with such incomprehensible vigor the shepherd whom she loves. The speeches of the following act, in which she explains her love and her necessary reserve in acting toward Aglante, are therefore more credible, and she gains our sympathy.

The author makes an even more striking modification in the character of the hero. The emphasis of the earlier Aglante is on service to the one he loves. His only duty, indeed his only honor, is to love her and serve her. This sentiment, showing the links of the pastoral to the chivalric code of conduct, is not present in Mairet's hero. Aglante does not want to serve Silvanire, he wants to be loved by her. Unlike the earlier hero he does not conceive of the five years he has faithfully loved her as a necessary period of unhappiness, an initiation by which he proves himself worthy of her love. D'Urfé's Aglante willingly suffers, believing that by doing so he is moving closer to eventual acceptance by the heroine. Mairet's Aglante is miserably unhappy, and only his natural reticence prevents him from outright complaints to Silvanire herself. Although he dare not tell her so, he believes that Silvanire is being unjust in not accepting his love, a criticism d'Urfé's hero would consider sacrilege. Constancy and perseverance are keys to Aglante's conduct, but service does not enter into his character.

The reason for the author's rejection of the service ethic in the creation of the hero is tied to his understanding of characterization. There is no character in Mairet's theater who combines suffering and complaining with the belief that such an attitude is service. Arimand of *Chryséide et Arimand* perfectly represents the character-type whose only existence is self-pitying sorrow, but he does not conceive of it as service to Chryséide. Florestan of *Sylvie* participates entirely in the service ethic, since he must literally earn his right to claim Méliphile. Suffering, however, plays no role in his character. Mairet seems to have considered the suffering role as essentially passive, and thus incompatible with service, which is essentially active. No character could both suffer and serve, be at the same time active and passive. The two attitudes are mutually exclusive.

One possible reason for the author's selection of d'Urfé's *Sylvanire* can be found in the similarities between its plot and those of Mairet's two earlier plays. At the base of the story one finds two young people in love and a conflict with parental interest. Both *Chryséide* and *Sylvie* begin with the same structure. The obstacle mentioned in the former is the same as in *Silvanire* —avarice and the father's desire to marry his daughter to a rich suitor. Although motivated by a different desire, more social than monetary, Sylvie's father likewise insisted that his daughter marry the man he was pleased to choose. The motif of conflict between parental right to dispose of children and filial duty to respect the parents' power appears in numerous plays of the period. The role of the parents has greater unity in *Silvanire*, however, than in *Sylvie*. Sylvie's parents in effect relinquish to the king their role as obstacle and do not appear after act II, scene 3. They have no place in the denouement. In *Silvanire* the heroine's parents are present throughout, the father pleading his case to the bitter end, in keeping with his irascible character. The Druids' decision concluding the play in favor of the young people parallels the king's conversion in *Chryséide*, as both endings stem from a superior power.

The subplots in *Sylvie* and *Silvanire* also show decided similarities. A shepherd is in love with the heroine—Philène with Sylvie, Tirinte with Silvanire—and she does not return his love. Furthermore, a shepherdess loves the shepherd—Dorise in *Sylvie*, Fossinde in *Silvanire*—and is united with him as the play ends. Again, this is an ending of complete convention. The addition of the chivalric subplot in *Sylvie*, Florestan's quest for Méliphile, underlines that play's debt to the romanesque aesthetic, an aspect which is absent from *Silvanire*, thereby allowing for greater unity.

Both pastoral tragicomedies entertain their audiences with scenes of magic and dreams. Macée's dream, foretelling future trouble for her daughter in *Sylvie*, is echoed in the dream of Silvanire, with an important difference. The dream of Sylvie's mother foretold an eventual happy outcome to the distressing situation; that of the latter heroine did not. The audience, attuned to the importance of dreams as signals of future events, has in *Silvanire* not been told about the final outcome but shares the heroine's perplexity until the situation is resolved. In this manner Mairet succeeds in creating some measure of dramatic suspense. While Macée presents both the conflict and its outcome, Silvanire poses an unresolved problem.

Both plays depend in large part upon magic, "the black art," for their endings. In effect Thélame and Sylvie, Aglante and Silvanire are joined thanks to the magic spells under which they fall. Although less spectacular than the final act of *Sylvie*, the scenes of magic in *Silvanire* serve a definite purpose. It is because she believes herself dying that the heroine admits her love and asks as a final request that she be allowed to marry Aglante. The illusion of the magic spell has unmasked a truth which had remained hidden. It has joined two lovers who were separated by a daughter's obligation to her parents and their exercise of parental authority. So strong are the feelings about the parent-child relationship that only in such dire circumstances could the daughter's true wishes be known and her desires granted. Magic thus plays a definite role in advancing the plot. Without harming her honor or going beyond the bounds that her modesty has prescribed, the heroine can admit her love.

The recourse to magic in both plays shows another trait common to works of this transitional period. The ending does not grow naturally from the situation or the characters as the author has portrayed them. Only a modified *deus ex machina* can bring the play to its conclusion. The king's conversion in *Chryséide*, despite its suddenness, is more believable than the miraculous magical endings of the two pastoral tragicomedies. The true conflict, rather than being logically answered, is simply submerged in the magic of the final acts. It is undoubtedly true that the audience expected and enjoyed these unreal scenes of magic. Mairet's ability to integrate them into the plot line shows his understanding of necessary cohesion in the dramatic work, more true for *Silvanire* than *Sylvie*. To some degree, though, in Mairet as in other writers, the dependence on magic to provide the denouement indicates a weakness, an inability to arrive at a believable conclusion with the material at hand. One can also argue that the play's progression from comprehensible reality to clouds of illusion and magic, and the eventual return to reality with the problem's solution, is evidence of the author's belief that some supernatural or superhuman intervention is necessary for the conclusion of a human problem. The author is not renouncing his artistic powers but subscribing to a mythical belief.

Mairet was of course following d'Urfé's plot line, though by his own decision. To refuse the magical ending would have necessitated reworking the entire play. Nonetheless, judging from the viewpoint of Mairet's complete work rather than this one play alone, it is likely that the use of the supernatural to bring about the necessary conclusion is evidence of the author's own belief, rather than simple dramatic convenience. The moral basis of the play, Mairet's own and not d'Urfé's, would seem to support this interpretation. The characters at times almost *preach* belief in the providence of heaven and the duty of man to accept blindly, without complaint and without sorrow, that which he cannot understand; for the greater powers will bring events to a fortunate conclusion if the characters merit it.

The unities in *Silvanire* represent, from the author's stated viewpoint, one of the play's primary interests. As did many authors anxious to publicize the fact that their dramatic creations held to the unity of time, Mairet has his characters take note of the time of day in their lines. At the beginning of act I Hylas remarks on the glorious break of day. The setting sun is mentioned at the end of act IV, and the beginning of act V takes place "before sunrise," according to Aglante. The play thus confines its action to the representation of twenty-four hours. Mairet emphasizes this in the preface, saying: "There is no single event (in the play) which could not realistically take place between two Suns."[13] The unity of place is likewise respected, within the less restrictive understanding of the rule than would later be applied. The action takes place in several different locations in Forez, all near the tomb of Silvanire, where the play reaches its conclusion.

The secondary interests and episodes which Mairet eliminated from the original play show his particular concern with the unity of action. The story has more cohesion, more functional unity than d'Urfé's version; it is simply Aglante and Silvanire's love for each other, which her parents will not allow. Tirinte presents the secondary plot line, but it is closely tied to the primary interest inasmuch as his actions, turning against him, bring about the union of the hero and heroine. In the preface Mairet explains that such episodes are "the instruments and the means necessary to lead the story to its conclusion with believability and propriety,"[14] and indeed it is Tirinte who unwittingly joins Aglante and Silvanire. The play is in perfect conformity to the unity of action as Mairet has defined it. Objections can be made, nonetheless, concerning those portions of the work whose existence is purely lyrical, in particular the prologue, the intermediary choruses, and the final two scenes of act V. There is no doubt that such interludes add little if anything to the action. They may, however, be seen as Mairet's acknowledgment of his debt to the Italians, a literary feature rather than a dramatic one, for in no other play does the author make use of the chorus.

Students of the genre have called *Silvanire* "the culmination of pastoral tragi-comedy in France."[15] Indeed it is one of the last works of the genre. In the early 1630s the pastoral and the pastoral tragicomedy were losing the interest of the public, whose tastes demanded more action and rejected the lyrical stance of those works clinging to the more static pastoral tradition. *Silvanire* can also be termed one of the best works of this genre. Sustained and unified in tone, written in accordance with the classical unities, a model of propriety, as actively dramatic as the chosen models would allow, the play represents a forward step for the theater of that period. It does look backward to the older genre and the passing influence of the Italian pastoral, but it also looks forward to the functional unity which the classical rules will bring, as they facilitate the concentration of interest and the heightened importance of the characters, their psychology, and their emotions. All of this will prove essential as French classical theater grows from these early works.

III Virginie

Although the unities had established their claim to the pastoral and to comedy before 1633, tragicomedy remained the exclusive property of the irregular school. At its origins a genre whose very nature was to escape in action the restricting bonds of time and space, tragicomedy symbolized, as it were, the limitless freedom of dramatic action demanded by those who refused the yoke of the rules. In 1632–33, however, Mairet wrote *Virginie*, his fifth play and first regular tragicomedy, thereby extending the hegemony of the classical limitations to the last stronghold of the irregulars.[16] Through the play's success he proved that the audience would accept a tragicomedy which conformed to the rules. He was not alone in doing so. Corneille's *Clitandre* (1632) was probably the first tragicomedy to hold to the twenty-four-hour rule. Boisrobert's *Pyrandre et Lisimène* (1632) respects the restrictions of time and space, although violating the unity of action.[17] Various other plays of such authors as Du Ryer and Rotrou show the general, though not generalized, movement toward acceptance of the unities and their application to tragicomedy.

Mairet expressed particular fondness for this play. The reason given takes on special significance when understood from the viewpoint of the opinions manifested in the preface to *Silvanire*. Eager that the public not confuse his heroine with the celebrated Roman Virginie, the author states that the story is entirely of his own invention. Mairet's position regarding the poet and allegiance to the unities is clearly evident here. Primary emphasis is on the poet's creation, his independence and his skill at inventing the characters and events which animate the dramatic poem. Debts to the ancients not withstanding, conformity to the specifics of the rules is secondary. It was not the success in adhering to the unities that pleased Mairet about *Virginie*, but rather the fact that the work was his creation of pure inventiveness.

Virginie[18] takes place in Byzance, a city in Thrace, which has just been conquered by rival troops from the neighboring kingdom of Epire. The last remnants of the defenders are besieged in a citadel in the city, while the rival court occupies the area. The main characters include Euridice, queen of Epire; her cousin Andromire; Amintas, a prince who is in love with the latter princess; and Harpalice, her old governess. Also attached to the queen's court are Périandre and Virginie, a young brother and sister who were discovered three months earlier shipwrecked on nearby shores. They have since been sheltered by the queen. Her main enemy, Cléarque, king of Thrace, also plays an essential role.

As the play opens, the audience learns of the recent victory over Cléarque and his troops, and of Périandre's exploits in battle. He and Virginie are praised as equals in beauty and virtue. In a later scene the two confide to each other that their feelings are more like those of lovers than brother and sister. The audience is thus given doubts about their true identity. Andromire, secretly in love with Périandre and torn between upholding her virtue and admitting her love, finally succumbs to passion. Unable and unwilling to control herself any longer, she tells Périandre of her love. As he flees, she decides to kill herself in order to purify her crime in her own blood. Having overheard the scene, Harpalice proceeds to make use of the knowledge to further her own ends. Dissuading the princess from suicide she claims to have heard Périandre boast not only of having captivated Andromire but the queen as well. With the help of Amintas they will accuse the queen of indecent conduct, thereby placing Andromire and Amintas on the throne. Harpalice also devises means of ridding them of Virginie and Périandre.

The plot to kill Périandre backfires as the awaiting assassins attack Harpalice's own son. Before expiring he warns Périandre, who arrived in time to drive off the hired killers, of the plot against him. The hero then decides to seek help from Cléarque, the besieged king, seeing him as the sole means of support against the machinations of the other court. The second plot also miscarries. Standing between two attackers, Virginie faints just at the moment when they reach her, and the two men kill each other. The key element of the plot, however, is put into action as the queen is accused of immorality.

A single combat will decide the truth or falsity of the accusations. Amintas supports the claims of the accusers; Périandre, incognito and freshly arrived from the citadel in the company of Cléarque, fights for the queen. He is victorious, and before dying Amintas admits the devised plot. Andromire asks to be exiled, and Harpalice is led away to be killed.

Not until the arrival of Calidor, a long lost old man, is the story finished. Explaining an ancient oracle and giving a confused story of astrological warnings, kidnappings, mistrust between neighboring countries, etc., he announces that Virginie is in actuality the daughter of Euridice, and Périandre the son of Cléarque. The play can thus end with acknowledgment of the call of blood, peace between nations, and marriage.

As is evident from the short plot summary, Mairet's play is nothing if not inventive. Although it does conform to the unities, it can be taxed on several accounts, the two most important being a weak structure and a general lack of verisimilitude. The oracle and necessary background elements are not introduced until the fourth act. The denouement lacks unity, as the Euridice story has no connection with the discovery of the true reality of the hero and heroine. There is an overabundance of "death bed" confessions. Périandre's decision to seek help from Cléarque strikes one as highly unbelievable, especially since it results in the abandonment of Virginie and the virtuous queen. The most unlikely event of all, Virginie's miraculous escape from death, is admitted by the author as unbelievable. Interestingly he makes use of this very lack of conceivable reality as an element of the plot. Harpalice presents it as proof of Virginie's magic powers, which she has already used, according to the old woman, to seduce the queen for her brother's pleasure. It is a spur to make Amintas and Andromire accept her decision to act against the queen, and it excuses Harpalice from responsibility for the plot's failure.

The play is not without its strong points. Though many of the events border on total unbelievability, the personages attest to Mairet's growing ability to create human characters. His inventiveness has served him admirably well in that respect. A key to this success is his power to express truly felt human emotion through his stage characters. On one level *Virginie* represents an exercise in the analysis of love, as three variations of the theme are examined. The mutual love of Virginie and Périandre is of the purest sort. The attraction of Andromire to Périandre presents a perfect example of love as seething violence turning to unbridled fury. Finally, the love of Amintas for Andromire is chivalric love, expressing itself through complete, unquestioning service and devotion.

Since Virginie and Périandre are supposedly brother and sister, it is natural that they be joined by ties of affection. Because of the strength of the emotion, however, doubt is cast upon the supposed sibling relationship. Some characters believe the professed familial tie to be false, as the two young people's origins are clouded by stories of foreign countries, a shipwreck, and a drowned father. Others, among them Harpalice, believe they have purposely disguised themselves in order to hide an illicit relationship behind a façade of purity and innocence. Even Virginie and Périandre question the true nature of their emotion and their ties. Analyzing their feelings they conclude that they surpass what sister and brother should feel. The question is openly stated between them, but believing love to be infinitely more violent and perhaps more dangerous than that which they feel, they decide it is not love. Fearing the fury of love they stand confident in their innocence. Their love remains pure, perhaps, because it is unnamed. Free of the conspicuous title it does not know the reproaches and guilt which the name "love" might bring. They accept the sentiment as a natural, though not entirely comprehensible, aspect of their relationship.

Andromire's love for Périandre and her subsequent admission of it violate virtually every moral convention in Mairet's theater—honor, *pudeur*, virtue, propriety. The love which inhabits Andromire is a fury, a passionate flame which her rational principles no longer control. "Fire" is the word most often used to describe her inner state; yet the blaze has not destroyed all sense within her. Her reasoning powers remain intact in total lucidity. Love is not madness for Mairet. Neither is Andromire helpless in her struggle against the fury, since she banishes virtue willingly and in complete consciousness chooses another path. The fault lies entirely within Andromire herself, and she is cognizant of that fact. Virtue is not absent, but voluntarily silenced. In addition, she experiences guilt, a result of lucidity remaining constant through the experience.

Realizing that her declaration of love has had no effect on Périandre, Andromire turns on the hero, forcing him to comprehend the price at which she has admitted her love. She cries out that his soul must know the great sorrow of her soul when she broke all barriers of modesty in order to tell him of her love. She bids Périandre look upon her without her high social station, simply as a woman in love. She tempts him with the crown, which might be hers and thus his, trying to snare him with promises of power, riches, position. All attempts fail, and Périandre's confusion grows. As he can no longer endure her mounting anguish nor answer her questions, he flees. Andromire realizes that in her confession she has broken every rule governing both her high social rank and her sex.

Immediately her only thought is for her honor. The princess has put herself in a desperate situation, having dropped all guard and admitted everything to a person lower than she. By means of a lie invented by Harpalice, she believes herself in imminent danger of being publicly ridiculed by Périandre. One word from him, and she will be completely and permanently

Mairet and Progress of the Unities

dishonored. The desperation of her situation and the volubility of her character force an immediate violent reaction. As Harpalice maneuvers her, Andromire comes to the realization that the only solution is to rid herself of Périandre. The lie by Harpalice suffices to catalyze the surging emotion and turn it to fury. To preserve her honor, that which after her love is most precious to her, she will allow anything.

Mairet shows fine psychological insight at this point, for Andromire's passion has not turned entirely to the fury of hate and vengeance. Some trace of love remains. The furious reaction was immediate and violent, but not long-lasting. Toward the end of her plotting with Harpalice she insists that the plan be executed quickly, for she fears that love returning will kill her desire for vengeance. The fury is mitigated, and for that reason more believable than pure anger.

Andromire's character shows traces of what will become the Racinian heroine. Her monologue of conflicting honor, shame, and passion gives indications of paths that Racine will follow. Her scene of admission and the ensuing cries of guilt bring to mind Phèdre and Hippolyte. Mairet's ability to observe, analyse, and translate sentiments into poetic lines of human truth reaches a high point in these scenes. Already evident in the earlier pastorals, especially *Sylvie,* this presentation of believable emotions ascends to a new range in *Virginie*—the tragic. The extent to which this is a key to Mairet's talent will be seen fully in his next play, the tragedy *Sophonisbe*.

Although an essential aspect of the characters and their relationships to one another, love does not stand as the highest value in *Virginie*. Even the strongest human emotions play a secondary role, as moral and religious criteria present the ultimate system of judgment. As in earlier plays, the characters' beliefs are strongly grounded in faith in providence. They have, moreover, totally rejected the earlier pessimism. Their faith is supported by an almost simplistic optimism, which stems from an unshakable belief that the superior powers will bring about a fortunate outcome to protect innocence and goodness. The strongest element of their faith is belief in the justice of heaven. This is the highest principle in the religious structure, and it is in order to give evidence to the existence of this principle that the lower powers—destiny, fate, gods—act within the world. All events on earth, whether mere quirks of fate or obvious acts of supernatural intervention, emanate from providence in order to prove heaven's justice. Finally, the characters believe that all acts move them closer to a predetermined end, which will be made known to them when it pleases the gods to do so.

Because of this strongly established and continuously affirmed religious basis, *Virginie* may be seen as a play depicting a struggle between religious and nonreligious forces, a morality play dramatizing the fight between good and evil. The play almost didactically shows the protection of the righteous and the punishment of evil doers. This principle is expressed very near the end of the play. Calidor, a priest figure, says: "Let this miracle forever perpetuate your deeds, Gods! whose justice has wrought such acts. Let the place and the day be forever glorified when you brought light from darkness and clearly showed to the eyes of the universe that your hands sooner or later punish those who do evil" (V. 6).

Following this principle the characters of *Virginie* can be divided into two distinct groups. In contrast to the earlier plays the division is not determined by age or by social class. The groups line up on strict moral grounds, the good versus the bad. Early in the play the rule is established, and by their words, actions, and associations the characters set themselves in one category or the other. On the side of good are Virginie and Périandre; Calidor, their tutor; Euridice, the queen; and Cléarque, her enemy, king of Thrace. Opposing them are Andromire, Harpalice, Amintas, and a host of secondary characters who assist them in the execution of their plots. Without exception those who act against the good characters are punished, whereas the cause of the innocent is upheld.

Virginie's virtue sets her apart even more than her physical beauty. She is esteemed by all who honor virtue and hated by those who would have virtue fall. Her role in the play is not active; she is the inspiration to action for those who support the cause of good through human deeds. In her role as inspiration Virginie does not place herself on a pedestal insisting upon service from those who would win her. She acts not from above but from within the group and most fully represents the internal force which motivates it.

While sharing her virtuous character Périandre functions primarily as the strength which upholds the cause of virtue. Supporting his physical and moral qualities as a *parfait cavalier* is "cette faim d'honneur" ("that hunger for honor"), as Virginie calls it. Périandre readily admits that his goal is honor. He is not the self-effacing hero fighting purely for others' causes. On a personal basis he has little reason to fight for Epire, being a foreigner who arrived there only some three months earlier. He is not motivated by patriotism or by a desire to gain the throne. In such areas Périandre is entirely disinterested. He seeks honor for himself and his sister.

Périandre represents a progression in Mairet's creation of the hero. Differing greatly from Arimand and Thélame, whose characters existed in word and inconclusive action rather than true accomplishment, the hero of *Virginie* continues the lineage begun in Florestan of *Sylvie*. He is the hero who unites action to his words and his emotions. But the principle which animates Périandre is different from the love which propelled Florestan to win Méliphile. In this respect Périandre's character undergoes a transition within the course of the play. In early scenes he is portrayed as the *chevalier* in search of honor, much as Florestan quested for glory. Later, he ascends to the role of defender of the right and becomes the representative of virtue in action. He moves beyond the world of political battles, and acts in a realm determined by the reigning moral criteria. In Périandre will be won or lost the struggle between good and evil.

Completing the side of good we find the two enemy monarchs. This may seem strange, but we must examine the characters from a moral, rather than a political, point of view. The moral considerations receive great attention in the first scene as Amintas describes the past battle. Although the army of Epire has succeeded in besieging and all but defeating the army of Thrace, the victors have nothing but praise for the valor and virtue of the enemy. On a political scale Cléarque is still the enemy, but on a moral scale he and his troops are not to be despised. Mairet's care in establishing this at the very beginning of the play shows his insistence that the characters not be judged along purely political lines as friend or foe.

This point is further strengthened by Périandre's decision (III. 5) to take refuge from his enemies and seek aid from Cléarque in the besieged citadel. As a political gesture this is absurdly unreasonable, but viewed as a moral move it makes great sense. Unable to find support in the one camp, he seeks it in the other. In this context Cléarque is not necessarily Périandre's enemy, and he can respond to the call for help in defending Euridice against a common enemy, evil. In the personal combat which climaxes the battle between the two forces, Cléarque acts as Périandre's second.

The concern for virtue as it overrules political considerations reappears after Périandre's victory. The king presents himself before Euridice, giving her the long-awaited occasion to exercise her vengeance on the man whom she has called "the odious Cléarque." She refuses, saying that he is no longer the same man for whose death she prayed to the gods. His great show of virtue has overcome her hate. Moral virtue surmounts political hatred, and the former enemies are united in marriage at the end of the play.

Harpalice is the character who most fully personifies evil in *Virginie*. She functions as the moving force behind the group we have named evil, as she alone brings ideas to strengthen its cause. She is solely responsible for the plots to kill Périandre and Virginie, to dishonor and dethrone the queen, and to place Amintas and Andromire in command of the kingdom. Her methods are fraud, lies, trickery, and malice. Her admitted purpose is to secure for herself and for her son places near the throne and the favors which would follow. Toward this end she manipulates her cohorts, understanding their own desires and preying on their weaknesses in order to draw them into closer alliance with her. Andromire, because of an ill-placed admission of love for Périandre, must protect herself from possible slander and dishonor. Deeply in love with the princess, Amintas will do anything to please her and win her. And so both become involved in the plot.

The accomplices of Harpalice in her plots do not totally share her identification with evil. Her nephew Zénodore expresses regret at being employed in "this unworthy task," namely, the murder of Virginie. Her son Philanax confesses the plot to Périandre, who has attempted to save him from his attackers. As they lie dying, both the son and the nephew fully recognize the right of heaven's justice, which has punished them for their misdeeds. The most unfortunate of the accomplices is the prince Amintas, who under different circumstances might have presented an example of the perfect hero. He is fully animated by love for Andromire; he is a brave and valiant knight and serves the crown honorably. His ambition is to make his loved one a queen, even more so than to make himself a king. Faith and courage at the service of love, glory at having served the mistress well, primary care for her above himself, and the knowledge that death is the greatest testimony of love—in these the chivalric code could not find more proper expression.

Two things destroy Amintas. First, the genre of the play—it is not a chivalric play where service counts above all but a morality play where the cause one serves weighs as much as one's dedication to the cause. In serving Andromire he is serving Harpalice and joining himself to a side which he knows to be far from totally truthful. In allowing his emotions to have full sway over his moral judgment, he betrays himself and becomes an active partner in the conspiracy. In the personal combat he is evil's representative and dies accordingly. Although not evil himself, he cannot avoid identification with the cause for which he is in battle. Second, his service to the loved one is misplaced in this play. He serves her before and above all else. The service would be correct in a play where love existed as the only law and the proper motive, but in *Virginie* the service of right surpasses even that of love. Only if one's love coincides exactly with right can it be respected. The prince could be the perfect active hero rendering service to the loved one, but a higher service is demanded, which is in contradiction to that which he pledges.

The moral, even moralistic, aim of the play is seen throughout, and heaven's justice destroys all persons who would transgress its rule. The fate of the characters who have died stands as a warning of the fate which awaits those who join forces with evil. The triumph of good speaks of the highest service which man can render, service to the right.

Having considered Mairet's fifth play, one away from the halfway mark in his career, we must ask ourselves what the work adds to our understanding of the author. One chief interest is the strength of his characterizations and his ability to draw varying portraits of believable human figures, ranging from the charming peasant Sylvie and the conniving sisters-in-law of the *Galanteries* to the passion of Andromire and the wickedness of Harpalice. The female characters stand out in high relief, often overshadowing the male characters by their very vitality. While not caricatures or flat personifications, the men generally fall into several types—the hero, active, passive, chivalric; the king; the jealous suitor, etc. It is in the creation of his female roles that Mairet shines, and *Virginie* gives ample evidence to the fact. Most importantly the tone of *Virginie*, as expressed especially through Andromire, points Mairet in the direction in which he will find his greatest success—the tragedy.

With the one exception of the comedy *les Galanteries du duc d'Ossonne* to be studied in the next chapter, Mairet based his earlier plays on already existent plots. Even *Sylvie* depended on other works for its structure. The author had thus worked with preconceived plans, altering them as his dramatic sense indicated, and he depended on his own invention more for character than for events. This borrowing from earlier sources was of course common practice throughout the century and in itself represents no fault. Mairet proved more than adept at adapting other works to his own needs and, in doing so, making them his own plays. *Virginie* shows, however, the pitfalls awaiting authors who free themselves from all dependence on others, insisting on total personal creation, within or without the limits of the unities. The structure of *Virginie*, of Mairet's own invention, has undeniable weaknesses—the double ending; poorly presented, overlong, and confusing exposition material; dependence on the most simplistic black and white morality for judgment of his characters. It can stand as no credit to him as a progressing dramatist in that respect. Further plays will show if structure is a major fault with Mairet's theater. For the present, *Virginie* stands as something of a failure in comparison to the excellent characterizations in the same play and the more than adequate structure of earlier works.

As a dramatic work whose claim to preeminence in literary history has been its respect for the classical unities, Mairet's *Virginie* clearly shows the rough form of the understanding of the rules in 1632–33. The action can take place at several different spots in one city without sinning against the unity of place. The play's unity of action shows its weakness in the double ending—one for Euridice, another for Virginie and Périandre. Mairet respects the unity of time but at the expense of believability. Nonetheless, we must not see this final point as a matter of criticism from the contemporary audience point of view. Some three years later, it was not the theatrical public which upbraided Corneille on many of the exact same counts— too much action in twenty-four hours and a general lack of verisimilitude—but the scholars and the other enraged authors. Mairet in his *Virginie* and Corneille in the *Cid* both give evidence of two basic truths. First, the tragicomedy, as the authors understood it, and respect due the classical unities were to prove all but mutually exclusive. Second, the public had not accepted as praiseworthy, let alone necessary, the limitations that the rules were eventually to bring. The unities had not yet won the public.

CHAPTER 4

Comic Interlude:
Les Galanteries du duc d'Ossonne

I Contribution to Comedy

ONLY recently have critics come to recognize the merits of Mairet's fourth creation and his only comedy, *les Galanteries du duc d'Ossonne, Vice-Roy de Naples.*[1] Because of a decided freedom in the characters' actions, not to mention a definite lack of scruples on the part of all, the play has been called immoral, obscene, licentious, and scabrous.[2] Such impulsive moral judgment has ignored the play's qualities—an intriguing and quickly moving plot, well-drawn characters, and a comprehension on the author's part of the necessity and uses of stage action. The play stands almost alone in the history of early seventeenth-century comedy as a precursor of Feydeauesque farce or Boulevard comedy, a sign of the paths comedy will take in centuries to come.[3]

The *Galanteries* is the first play in which Mairet portrays a historic figure as protagonist. Born in Valladolid, Spain, Don Pedro Girón, duke of Osuna, was named in 1615 viceroy of Naples after numerous successful campaigns in Flanders and Sicily. Because of his immense popularity in Naples, Philip IV, king of Spain, grew suspicious of him and ordered his return to Spain, where the duke was arrested. He died in prison in 1624, possibly poisoned. He had been a great favorite of France's Henri IV and came to be known to the French through Tallemant's account of various of his "bons mots et naïvetés."[4] For his play Mairet retained the duke's reputation for humor, as well as the setting, Naples.

It was long thought that a play entitled *Las Mocedades del duque de Osuna* by Cristobál Monroy y Silva served as Mairet's primary source in the composition of the *Galanteries*.[5] This thesis has been discounted, because the Spanish play in all likelihood postdates the French comedy. It seems possible, however, that Mairet knew of certain incidents in the life of the real duke, because an Italian biography published in 1699 recounts an amorous adventure that parallels the plot of Mairet's work. The biographer relates that the duke obliged a friend in need of shelter from his wife by sending him to a house three miles away. He properly takes advantage of the situation by visiting the friend's wife late at night, being welcomed not only by the wife, but by her mother as well.[6] The Don Juan character of the duke seems then a matter of reality rather than artistic invention.

Having lost all gaiety and pleasure in the court's normally joyous pastimes, the duke admits to his servant, Almédor, that this unnatural melancholy is due to love. He has fallen under the spell of a beauty whom he noticed at the theater. Paulin, a friend of the duke, enters and requests his assistance in escaping the city. He is suspected of attacking and seriously wounding Camille, a rival for his wife's affections. The duke allows Paulin to stay temporarily in his country house thirty miles away. The situation proves an unexpected blessing for the duke, as it is Paulin's wife, Emilie, of whom he became enamored at the theater. Before leaving Naples Paulin visits his wife, accusing her of grieving for his rival's demise rather than for her husband's departure. He is not mistaken, and he instructs his sister, Flavie, a young widow, not to let Emilie out of her sight.

Standing near Flavie's house one cold evening, the duke is startled when he notices a man climb down a silk ladder from an upper window and then climb back up reentering the house. The duke follows and discovers Emilie dressed as a man. Although he tells her of his passion, she says that she still loves Camille. She asks that he take her place in bed next to her old decrepit sister in order to allow her to visit Camille and inquire of his health. Obliging her, the duke soon discovers that Flavie is neither old nor decrepit, but a beautiful young angel. Furthermore, she has spied the earlier scene, knows his identity, and feigns speaking aloud in a dream in order to let him know that she loves him. As the scene ends, she is under her covers, and because of the cold she allows the duke to share her bed, insisting that he remain on top of the covers. Honor must prevail. When Emilie returns, however, the duke tells her nothing of his encounter with Flavie, just as Flavie has decided to tell her brother nothing of his wife's adventures. The duke decides that it is only proper that he win both ladies, musing that a comedy could be written of his escapades.

In the meantime, Camille has recovered and undergone a change of heart. He no longer loves Emilie but rather Flavie. In speaking to his servant Octave, he concocts a story of vengeance in order to cover the somewhat sudden and unbelievable turn of events. He instructs Octave to give a note with some money to Stephanille, Flavie's maid. Emilie shortly thereafter learns from her father that rumors are being spread about her, and she suspects the duke of having bragged too freely. Fearing her sister-in-law may hear of her supposed relationship with the duke, and knowing Flavie to be in love with him, Emilie shows her various notes which the duke has sent her. She asks her advice on the situation. Flavie responds in sort by showing her Camille's note which Stephanille has just delivered. The ladies decide to take separate bedrooms. In the final act both Camille and the duke arrive at the house at night, Camille seeking Flavie and the duke Emilie. They are led to the wrong bedrooms, and soon the four characters embark on a discussion of fidelity and the double standard. The women ask why they should honor a code which the men disregard with such impunity. A general pardon is granted, and the four are about to sit down to supper when a servant announces Paulin's imminent arrival. He is soon dislodged thanks to the duke's stratagem and Paulin's cowardice, and the two couples—the duke and Flavie, Emilie and Camille—can continue their pleasures.

The existence of only one comedy in Mairet's work leads to the obvious question: why did he write it? One answer lies in the young author's desire to try his talent in all possible genres, and by the end of his career Mairet had written works in the tragic, tragicomic, pastoral, and comic veins. Another more immediate reason for Mairet was Corneille's success in comedy, an accomplishment which the more established author's pride must have felt the need to equal. Corneille's *Mélite*, a success for Montdory's troupe in 1629, did much to reestablish literary comedy in the eyes of the public. Mairet doubtless hoped to profit from the renewed interest, and it seems that his comedy enjoyed a healthy success. A final consideration which may have entered the author's mind was the troupe that logically would perform his next play, that of Montdory and Le Noir, supported by the comte de Belin, Mairet's new protector. They had excellent comic actors and had already staged Corneille's comedies.

Mairet's *Galanteries* represents a forward step in the renewal of interest in comedy as opposed to farce in the first third of the seventeenth century. According to Scherer, only six plays were called comedies between 1610 and 1629.[7] Indeed it can hardly be affirmed that comedy as a literary genre truly existed in French theater at that time. Several reasons for this paucity of comic plays can be advanced. The farcical actors at the Hôtel de Bourgogne satisfied the public's desire for gaiety and their need to laugh, improvising coarse, unrefined comic sketches, and consequently there existed no strong desire on the part of the audience for a more refined literary comedy. Only after the deaths of the three main farce actors and the resultant gradual decline in interest in farce could authors respond to any public interest in comedy. In addition to farce, the pastoral and tragicomedy often possessed comic elements. Mairet's *Chryséide et Arimand*, for example, contains two scenes with innkeepers which are properly comic in contrast to the more sustained lyricotragic tone of the rest of the play. His *Sylvie*, through observation and portrayal of lifelike characters, gives early indications of what will later become the *comédie de moeurs* ("comedy of manners"). Furthermore, the Spanish sources, which were to provide the plot structures and incidents of so many comedies written after 1640, had not yet been mined to any great extent.

The French comedies of the late 1620s and 1630s—those of Corneille, Mairet, Du Ryer, Rotrou—stand as individual experiments, but they by no means constitute a school. No single work exercised determining influence on the course of the genre, although their public success, coupled with the diverse directions taken by the authors, showed the way to later development of the various comic modes—comedy of intrigue, comedy of character, and comedy of manners. The essential feature of the period's comedies is their role in the necessary renewal of interest in the genre. They serve as well as indications of its progression from a merely popular diversion to the future classical comedy, *la grande comédie*.

Mairet's contribution to the genre illustrates the separation from the French farce. The poet includes none of the stock characters so familiar to the audience of the Hôtel de Bourgogne. No pedantic doctors, no drunken valets, no amorous old fools enliven the stage. Likewise the source of humor is not the broad physical action of the *farceurs*. No scenes of domestic battles and misguided blows, such as Molière inserted in his comedies, can be seen in the *Galanteries*. It is nonetheless true that the initial base of the play, a wife deceiving her cruel husband by taking a lover, betrays ties both to the farce and to the Italian *commedia dell'arte*. As though acknowledging the author's debt to the latter, Camille in act V, scene 6 calls Paulin "Pantalon."

The comedy is much more in the style of the Italian *novelle*, which were popularized in France at that time. It also shows traces of the Spanish influence, although in general being less romanesque than those comedies based on Spanish sources. The structure of the play reflects this duality of influences—the action takes place in Italy, but the main character is Spanish.[8]

II Analysis of the Play

Les Galanteries du duc d'Ossonne is primarily a comedy of intrigue born of the hedonistic search for pleasure. In its use of disguises and trickery, the complexity of its action and its portrayal of love as sheer sensual pleasure, the comedy continues the general lines of the Italian spirit. There reigns an atmosphere of unrestrained freedom, and the spirit behind that freedom is a healthy, almost ebullient cynicism. The characters derive pleasure not only from the conquest but from the chase as well, imparting the baroque ideal of truth as movement and action to the greater part of the play, and resulting as well in the Don Juanesque character of those concerned.[9] As a comedy of intrigue, the play might be considered just another scenic romp were it not for the comedy's characters. They exist not only because of the action but apart from it, standing as believable characters endowed with vitality and life. The cruel and cowardly husband, the two guileful women, the scheming servants—every character possesses distinguishing characteristics and exists as a separate creation, remaining true in word and deed to the individual identity. Such believable characters are striking in their modernity. One thinks of the nineteenth-century French bedroom farce or the twentieth-century boulevard comedy, with lively characters bent on pursuing pleasure through a complex and intriguing variety of incidents. The veracity of the characters, based on the author's observations of his contemporaries, and the wealth of elements of daily life found in the play almost succeed in making of it a comedy of manners. The duke mentions his scented gloves and sachets with which to combat offensive odors. He has a watch which strikes the hour, inopportunely waking Flavie in act II, scene 3. The characters communicate by means of letters sealed with wax and silk. Stephanille, Flavie's servant, complains of the outrageous prices at the market. Despite the *imbroglio* and *invraisemblance* of certain situations, the finesse of Mairet's observations and the reality of his creations in the comedy never fail to show through.

In creating his fourth play Mairet abandoned the pastoral tragicomic vein in which he had written his first three plays. At the most basic level the comedy seems a complete break with the earlier plays. The previously drawn character types are absent, as are the polarities and the resulting conflicts of the pastoral tragicomedies. The values of the earlier characters—love and honor—seem forgotten in the exuberance of the comedy. Taking the same values, Mairet has restated them in a different context. He remolded them to fit the comedy, as they in essence ask the same questions, but call for reexamination and new answers.

Love in the earlier plays was conceived as the motivating power from which the characters' actions, both verbal and physical, sprang. It supplied both the energy within them and the final goal toward which this force impelled them. The concept of love as a power possessing the individual occurs also in the *Galanteries*. In the first scene Almédor notes a strange change in his master's personality. Formerly gay, he has become melancholy and pensive, and he no longer shares the joy with which he used to animate the court. Almédor concludes, "Love which changes all things has caused this metamorphosis in your character" (I. 1). The duke can only agree saying, "I am visibly dissimilar to myself." Love has wrought this change in the duke. The vocabulary used to describe the emotion—fire, passion, love born of a glance—may lead to the assumption that the treatment of love resembles that of the pastorals. We are, however, concerned with a different genre. In the comedy it is the exteriorization of love, the appearance it produces in the characters and the actions it causes them to perform, which is of prime importance. Love as an inner feeling, a sentiment motivating the character to expression of that love in words or action, does not enter into play.

Almédor points out the appearance which love has inflicted on the duke. "Dreamy as a poet with your haggard face, languishing eyes and your skin yellow with love," the duke seems quite ridiculous. Rather than combat his valet's mockery, the duke laughs and agrees with him. This agreement and the absence of a telling defense of his condition distinguish the duke from the earlier lovers, and the comic treatment of love from that of the pastorals. Almédor's argument—that if one has no hope, if the ill is greater than the possible good, and if the unfortunate person still persists in loving, he is a fool—is similar to arguments presented to Arimand by Bellaris. But the duke's answer, "the greatest wisdom is folly in love," acknowledging the madness, differs greatly from Arimand's defense of his hopeless, helpless situation. Love never totally recovers from such mockery in the *Galanteries*.

Honor, a virtue which remained intact in the pastorals, appears in terms of the same exterior-interior duality. Honor for Sylvie and Silvanire signified an inner virtue which set limits that they could not transgress. This definition of honor is not applicable to the female characters of the comedy. In discussing her liaison with Camille, Emilie says, "We have been too lucky and too careful to let ourselves be caught in a situation which would compromise our honor" (II. 3). Having been careful to avoid discovery, she preserves her honor, because only she and her lover know of their amorous escapades. By "honor" Emilie means reputation, the exterior indication of a supposed inner virtue. In a later scene, fearing that the duke has informed Flavie of their affair, thus ruining her in the eyes of a third party, she cries out, "Discovered and lost as well as in love! Alas! my honor is abandoned" (V. 6). This overpowering anxiety about the opinions of others and the concern for keeping up appearances shows the main interest again to be mere reputation. Honor, the virtue of which reputation should be the sign, is absent, and we have an exterior which is not supported by an interior truth. The characters are not so much interested in being honorable as in appearing so. Emilie's father, hearing news of her liaison with Camille, comes to warn his daughter, "You are innocent, or you ought to be; but it matters even more that you appear so" (IV. 4). The verbs "to be," "ought to be," and "appear" note a progression from true being to mere semblance. If Emilie is not honorable, she should at least present a show of honor. Her renown must stand, though it be the pretense of an absent virtue.

Were any of the characters unaware that professed goodness merely masked the absence of true virtue, there could be a conflict between appearance and reality as found in pastorals, but such is not the case. None of the characters is fooled by appearances or tricked into accepting them as real. They do not play the roles of deceiver and deceived, for there is no true deception. All characters operate with full knowledge of each others' motives and desires. The pretense of virtue is simply an element of the game in which all participate. Furthermore, even the pretense of goodness is dropped and the characters belie their virtuous words by nonvirtuous actions whenever the occasion arises.

What then is the game, its means, and its goal? The characters are engaged in a search for pleasure, an amoral though not licentious game of sexual intrigue. Free of social or moral constraints, they are pure hedonists, taking joy both in the intricate game they play as they move toward the desired relationship and in its accomplishment. The means to the end are deceit, trickery, and falsification of reality, all leading ultimately to comedy.

The characters misrepresent themselves to others and are ready at all times to deceive one another in thought, word, and deed—mental attitude, language, and action. Such key verbs as *jouer* ("to play"), *tromper* ("to deceive"), and *feindre* ("to pretend") recur frequently, as deceit forms the very tissue of their game. Flavie says speaking of her sister: "Il me faut...tromper cette trompeuse" ("I must deceive that deceiver") (IV. 12). Speaking of his wife and her infidelity, Paulin decides: "Puisqu'elle feint feignons pareillement" ("Since she's pretending, let's pretend as well") (I. 5). The goal is to hide or disguise the truth from all undesirable parties by presenting a false exterior which they are to accept as real. At some time or other in the course of the play virtually all the characters have recourse to deception, by out and out lying, by simply omitting to tell the truth, or by appearing to be something which they are not. In the *Galanteries* there are twenty scenes which are essentially dialogues. In fifteen of them one or both characters act or speak in a manner which may be described as trickery. All characters except Emilie's father, who appears in one scene, make use of these means. The reason for the father's abstinence is simply that he does not participate in their search for pleasure, and thus he has no reason for recourse to ruse.

The ruling attitude of the game can be seen in Camille's line "Quel crime aurai-je fait pourvu qu'elle l'ignore?" ("What crime will I have committed as long as she does not know it") (IV. 2). A crime is no crime unless the person against whom it is directed knows it as such. The truth of an action, or, by extension, of an appearance, is not determined by the party who performs it but by the person who perceives it. Discovery alone creates crime.

Motivation for action presents another essential duality in the characters. At first reading they appear entirely motivated by self-interest, each individual acting in his own behalf at the expense of all others, with the sole concern being personal gain. As the duke says, "I don't do anything for nothing" (III. 2). At other times, however, he professes the desire to help others

Comic Interlude ...

even to his own detriment. The seeming disinvolvement is quickly recognized as a trick to gain confidence and trust. Promising in a later scene to help Emilie in her efforts to see her wounded lover, Camille, the duke realizes that if Camille should die "my service will be rewarded" (III. 2). His unselfishness is unmasked as a desire for personal gain.

The quest for self-satisfaction is, however, not without bounds. If the characters based their efforts purely on self-interest, they would resort to anything in order to further their personal cause. Individual contentment would present the ultimate goal, no matter what the inconvenience to others. This would lead to the tyranny seen in figures of power in the earlier plays, but such an attitude is absent from the *Galanteries*. All the characters understand that no relationship can be consummated except by mutual consent. The duke says to Emilie, "I will never approve that cowardly desire to rule love with tyranny" (II. 4). At that point he expresses a fundamental truth behind the game in which all are engaged. Nothing can be accomplished without the consent of both parties. Indeed the duke's first words to Emilie are that he will retire immediately if he is inconveniencing her. She of course allows him to stay. When two characters establish a relationship, the desire for personal gain is restrained by considerations for the partner. Trickery, although an essential part of the game, is directed either by a couple against a third party or by an individual against another individual outside the mutual relationship. One partner never purposely tricks the other in hopes of being able to force the issue.

In one instance the game becomes deadly serious, and Mairet adds a new element to his theater. The cry is vengeance, arising when someone so seriously infringes on the rules of the game that the carefully prepared and supported exterior is in imminent danger of collapse. When she learns that her husband has physically attacked and possibly killed her lover, Emilie girds herself for battle, and her lines of passion ring surprisingly true when compared with the artifice and empty eloquence of other scenes. The only previous mention of vengeance in Mairet's theater was the inexplicable violence with which Fossinde attacked Tirinte when he refused her love in *Sylvie*. The only explanation given in the earlier play is that unrequited passion often turns to hatred. The vengeance in the *Galanteries* is much more carefully explained and its verbal expression more comprehensible than Fossinde's mad diatribes. Emilie, moreover, is not the only character to cry for vengeance. Flavie does so for the harm done her brother, Emilie's husband. In addition, Camille feigns vengeance upon Flavie to redress the wounds her brother inflicted on him.

Vengeance represents a form of satisfaction for such wrongdoings. Early in the play Emilie says that she is living only to die satisfied and avenged. She wants to perform a famous act of vengeance for the attack on her lover, but says that an obscure one would suffice to put her in the right. For all this violent verbalizing, physical expression of vengeance is never attempted during the play. The only encounter is the one between Camille and Paulin before the play begins. Emilie's vengeance results in nothing even vaguely approaching anyone's death, and Camille's remains pure show. The most telling comment on vengeance within the play comes from the duke: "What a strange thing to see how animosity stifles generosity in us, and that here more than elsewhere outraged friends want to be avenged by such cowardly acts" (I. 2). He reacts as a player shocked at the behavior of his fellow players. The dead seriousness of their intent strays beyond the bounds of the rules which circumscribe their attitudes. A completely honest desire for vengeance threatens to destroy the structure of harmless illusion that supports the game while providing the accepted means by which the characters move toward realizing their pleasure. While it may seem strange to hear the duke characterize the attitudes of the characters as *générosité*, there is a reason behind his choice of that word. The characters act according to rules known and accepted by all. They employ the same means toward the same end, refusing to force their desire on others or to triumph at the expense of an unwilling player. He who wins has simply played the best game. The only characters who are punished or beaten at the game are those who deserve it, in particular the cowardly husband anxious to force his will upon his wife. In a perhaps perverse sense this is a kind of *générosité*, an accepted moral, or amoral, pattern and code in which those who follow the rules receive their just reward. Vengeance does not

Comic Interlude ...

belong to the game nor can it have a role in a play that portrays the machinations of characters involved in a search for pleasure. It remains foreign to the nature of the *Galanteries*, being the only departure from the cynical cheerfulness which forms the tone of the play, an early seventeenth-century form of gamesmanship.

III Comedy and the Unities

Standing chronologically after the regular pastoral tragicomedy *Silvanire*, the comedy is striking by the almost total disregard for the unities. This is not a sign of conscious rejection on the part of the author, but rather an indication that at this period of their existence the rules were not automatically applied to all dramatic creations. Mairet had not delivered an ultimatum in the preface to *Silvanire*; he was consciously stating an ideal to be sought. It was not until five years later, after the catharsis of the quarrel of the *Cid*, that the rules would earn their title to dramatic necessity. As for the unity of time in the *Galanteries*, the action takes place over a period of at least three days, the time in excess of the actual presentation passing between the acts, but not between scenes of a single act. The author respects the unity of place as understood during the period 1630-40. Mairet limits the action to one city, more specifically to three houses, those of the duke, Flavie, and Camille, and an open square contiguous to all three.

The play demands an entirely new definition of the unity of action. That definition might be the following: given four characters, two male and two female, examine and portray all the possible pleasurable combinations. Whether we call it unity of pleasure, the hedonistic spirit, or unity of movement, we are dealing with the baroque aesthetic of truth in movement rather than stability, and the play may be considered an exhaustive study of combinations, moves, and subsequent changes on both the physical and emotional levels in four characters. Mairet accomplishes this in three situations.

The first situation finds the duke seeking to seduce Emilie, Flavie in love with the duke, and Emilie and Camille in a mutually accepted liaison. The element precipitating the initial change is the jealous Paulin, who, once he has played that role, can conveniently take his leave. The resulting situation two shows the duke anxious to conquer both women. Camille has changed allegiance and now wants Flavie. The two women still hold to the original partner, but both willingly accept advances from the other man. The final situation, when all previous moves have been brought into the open, joins the duke with Flavie and reunites Emilie and Camille. Paulin makes one final appearance in an attempt to regain his wife but succeeds only in earning a second banishment. The amorality of the play is evidenced by the fact that the only legally constituted relationship, that of Paulin and Emilie as husband and wife, is the first to be broken and is never repaired. The rule is movement toward satisfaction; the two accepted truths are again action and pleasure, often merging into one. In that statement can be found the only unity of the play—the characters' enjoyment of their pursuits and conquests, the audience's delight in the vivacious animation of the scenic action.

CHAPTER 5

The Tragedies

I Introduction: The State of Tragedy Before Mairet

IN its earliest stages seventeenth-century French tragedy underwent the influence of two distinct literary forms. The first was the humanistic tragedy of the Renaissance, which had found its greatest exponent in Robert Garnier. Following the example of Seneca, authors conceived tragedy as the spectacle of an illustrious misfortune, pathetic in tone and morally significant. All interest concentrated on the main character, the victim of a terrible catastrophe, crushed by fate or by human cruelty. Writers of tragedy did not invent subjects for their plays but drew them from the Bible, lives of saints, Greek or Roman history, and more recent history. Examples are Grevin's *Caesar* (1561), Jean de la Taille's *Saül* (1562), Garnier's *Hippolyte* (1573) and *les Juifves* (1582), and Montchrestein's *L'Escossaise* (1601), a play about Mary, Queen of Scots. Since the stage action consisted primarily of the complaints and lamentations of the victim and those around him, Renaissance tragedy remained static in character, and lyrical and oratorical in tone rather than dramatic. Any active event took place off stage and was later recounted by a messenger. This understanding of tragedy, with its single victim powerless against destruction by a greater force and its resulting stress on the lyricopoetic element, proved disadvantageous to any true dramatic portrayal. Tragedy, as defined and practiced at that time, and drama, in the sense of the exposition of an active conflict, were incompatible.

In form the Renaissance tragedy conformed generally to the unities. Authors wrote their plays in five acts and took care not to shock the public morality. They introduced choruses at the end of each act whose function it was to comment on the preceding action and draw a moral lesson for the audience. Such artificial devices as premonitions, dreams, and ghosts abounded in order to create the proper atmosphere of fear, so that the spectators might appreciate the lesson.

In reaction to the static tragedy of the Renaissance, the irregular, or baroque, tragedy came into being.[1] This presented the second important influence on early seventeenth-century tragedy. Without greatly changing the exterior form of the genre, dramatists infused their "new" tragedy with the very element that the earlier tragedy lacked, namely, action. Desirous of pleasing a public whose tastes demanded more than just the declamation of pathetic woes, authors showed their audience the events from which those pleas resulted, often going to excesses and presenting instances of murder, rape, incest, and adultery. Primary interest centered on the violence and variety of stage action. Under the pressure of these new additions, the form gradually began to give way as well. The chorus disappeared, the oratorical tirades were shortened in order to allow for more rapid dialogue, and the unities, as well as the proprieties, were no longer respected.

The irregular tragedy was representative of a general enlargement in the scope of drama—in the representation of action, time, and place, as well as in the form used by authors to contain their actions. This period likewise witnessed the birth in France of the tragicomedy, the pastoral, and the various combinations of both. All these genres, which came into being shortly before the beginning of the century, represent a substantially new direction taken by theater, one which would be of great importance for the development of theater in seventeenth-century France and for tragedy in particular.

The theater of Alexandre Hardy, who began writing roughly in 1592, represents the first important collection of plays attributed to one author writing specifically for the approval of the theatrical public.[2] Since Hardy was a *poète à gages*, a dramatist directly employed by a theatrical troupe to provide them with plays, his works necessarily reflect the influence of the public's desires concerning dramatic production. He wrote for the troupes of Valleran-le-Comte and Bellerose at the Hôtel de Bourgogne, and later for Villiers, the director of the "Vieux Comédiens du

The Tragedies

Roi." His published works include twelve tragedies, although he is believed to have composed many more. In his tragedies Hardy conformed generally to the humanist doctrine of the genre. He took his subjects from ancient history, many coming from Plutarch. The tragedies were divided into five acts and were written in alexandrines. The author made use of the chorus, as well as other conventions like dreams, prophecies, and premonitions.

Hardy had stated that he wanted to preserve the literary tradition of the Renaissance. However, the spirit which animates Hardy's tragedies differs greatly from the sorrowful lamentations and pitiful destruction of a passive victim found at the base of the Renaissance tragedy. Be it a concession to the desires of the public or an expression of his own aesthetics, the soul of the author's tragedies is that of the irregular tragedy. In his work the tragedies resemble the tragicomedies to the extent that it sometimes proves difficult to separate the two genres. Both are imbued with action, atrocious and varied, and exaggerated violence of emotions. His characters are driven by violent passions. No longer the victims of insurmountable powers, they refuse to be the playthings of destiny. This change in the conception of characterization was seconded by a basic change in Hardy's understanding of what drama should properly represent. As the heroes were active, some element had to exist against which their action could be measured. Tragedy, then, was no longer the static representation of an unfortunate situation, but the portrayal of a struggle between two violent adversaries. The crux of tragedy began to be humanized. The emphasis of the genre on the opposition between man and the will of heaven ended, and man himself provided the principal dramatic interest, often by the sheer passionate willpower of the characters portrayed.

After the theater of Hardy the next important step taken by tragedy was Théophile's *Pyrame et Thisbé*. Written most likely in 1621, the work was published in 1623. In the history of tragedy Théophile's play represents a forward step in the realm of style more than in concerns of form. Reacting against the harsh hyperbolic style of earlier writers, in particular Hardy, the poet wanted to create a more modern, more refined style. By its simplified, unified composition and by the beauty of Théophile's poetic line *Pyrame et Thisbé* helped orient tragedy and drama in general toward a more modern representation of sentiments.[3]

In the years after 1625 the overwhelming popularity of the tragicomedy and the pastoral all but totally eclipsed the tragedy. Under the influence of the Spanish, the genre was oriented toward melodrama and the "romanesque." Historic tragedy was for all intents dead. Authors no longer proved their talents with a tragedy, but with a pastoral or a tragicomedy sure to excite audience interest. Free rein was given to liberty, to the action which the public demanded, and there was consequently no room for the more measured tragedy. The older genre could not provide the pleasure which writers of the irregular genres claimed to be the sole purpose of theater. The authors of that time had in effect lost the notion of tragedy.[4] The element which they had eliminated from Renaissance tragedy in the new understanding of the genre was the belief that the play should expose some truth, some moral or religious lesson. Dramatists of the early seventeenth century placed macabre or extraordinary action at the heart of the tragedy, thereby all but equating it with tragicomedy. Action *per se* was considered sufficient motivation for drama.

The quarrel of the unities in the late 1620s and early 1630s marked the beginning of the rebirth of tragedy. By presenting an alternative to the irregular genres, the theoreticians initiated the movement toward tragedy's acceptance by the authors and hopefully by the public. Rather than presenting the rules as unquestionable dogma necessary to the production of good literature, the scholars justified them according to intellectual proprieties and good taste. In addition, the rising Italian influence gave impetus to the movement away from the irregular genres. Interestingly, Mairet played a role in both camps. His first two plays, especially the great success of the pastoral tragicomedy *Sylvie* (1626), helped orient the theater of the mid and late 1620s toward the irregular genres. In 1629–30 with his regular pastoral *Silvanire* (1629) he presented a work which would help bring about the acceptance of the unities and prepare the dramatic terrain for tragedy. Mairet's *Sophonisbe* (1634) was to continue his role as an innovator, this time in pure tragedy.

The Tragedies

Before examining the play itself there remains one question which merits discussion. With the rage of the irregular genres in the early 1630s and the seemingly unflagging popularity of action-filled "romanesque" drama, how did it happen that within the space of two months two regular historical tragedies were written, one of which proved popular enough to help reorient the course of the theater? Rotrou's *Hercule Mourant*, inspired by Seneca, and Mairet's *Sophonisbe*, both presented in 1634, appeared at a time when one would have least expected tragedies. There exists a tie between the two works, and it supports what has been said earlier about the importance of protectors and the dramatic theoreticians. That tie is Chapelain.

Chapelain had helped rescue Rotrou in 1632 from his position as *poète à gages* with the Hôtel de Bourgogne, thereby ensuring him some measure of independence. Along with the comte de Fiesque, and the comte de Belin, he served as protector for Rotrou. Since Chapelain's position in the quarrel of the unities is clearly known, it seems logical to assume either that he asked Rotrou to compose a regular tragedy or that the author decided to do so himself in recognition of Chapelain's benefits. The *Segraisiana* also indicates that the initiative for Mairet's tragedy came from Chapelain.[5] It does not seem unlikely that the scholar suggested the subject of the play to Mairet.[6] The author's willingness to please his protectors and those in a position to aid him is known and totally comprehensible. The impetus toward creation, as was often the case in Mairet's career, came perhaps from above, and as a loyal, faithful courtesan he obeyed to the best of his abilities. Fortunately, this instance produced Mairet's best and most influential theatrical work. For that he could thank his talents which had matured sufficiently to allow him to prove himself more than equal to the task.

II Sophonisbe

The play[7] takes place in Cirtha, capital city of Numidia in North Africa, a kingdom which at the opening of the play is at war with an allied army of Roman and African troops. Syphax, the old king, had earlier deposed the rightful king, father of Massinisse, and also forced Asdrubal, king of Carthage, to give his daughter, Sophonisbe, to him in marriage. It is primarily the queen's hatred of Rome which has caused Syphax to war against the greater power, for he had previously sought and gained Rome's friendship. Massinisse has joined with the Romans in order to reconquer the kingdom and win the throne which rightly belongs to him. After his victory Numidia would become a province under Roman hegemony.

In the first scene Syphax berates his young queen for betraying both the love he shows her and their honor as reigning sovereigns by collaborating with Massinisse, their common enemy. Having discovered a letter supposedly addressed to the warrior, Syphax believes Sophonisbe to be in love with him. Not content with causing him to lose all glory and fortune in the political realm, she now betrays her husband's honor as well as her own, he says. She tries in vain to defend herself but only succeeds in embittering the king all the more.

In a monologue following the quarrel Syphax rues the day he set eyes on Sophonisbe. Her charms deprived him of all control over himself. His reason and will, his power of judgment, were held powerless in the sway of the passion he felt for her. Blaming her he blames himself as well for the sudden change in fortune which followed their marriage. As he prepares for battle with Massinisse, he wishes the worst possible fate for his enemy—may he some day have Sophonisbe as his wife.

The queen's own feelings become known in the next scene. She does love Massinisse and suffers because he does not know of her love. Her servant Phénice assures her that her physical beauty is enough to win any man. Sophonisbe herself is frightened by the passion she feels and by the destiny which pursues her. Realizing that her love is a crime, she speaks of the "illegitimate fire" burning inside her. As her servant girls watch the battle from a high tower, descending periodically to report on the events, Sophonisbe delivers a monologue which enlightens the audience on her confused state of mind. She pleads that her reason not allow her heart to hope for an enemy victory. She is torn between the desire to conserve her glory at the expense of Massinisse's life and her desire to see him

The Tragedies

live so she may love him. The queen's fear of Roman domination equals her ardor for the warrior. The gods are tired of her happiness, she says. They have lit the fires within her as a punishment for some unknown crime against love or heaven.

Hearing of the death in battle of her husband, Sophonisbe considers him fortunate at having died and not known life as a conquered monarch. She would prefer death to the shame of living enslaved. She is tempted by suicide, which she believes to be less shameful a fate and more worthy of human courage. Phénice and Corisbe suggest that she attempt to win Massinisse's affection. They assure the queen that her sorrow makes her even more attractive and that Massinisse will both love and respect her.

As they predicted, the conquering hero is vanquished by Sophonisbe. After pitying her misfortune and assuring her that he will not misuse his newly won power, Massinisse is slowly entranced by her beauty. He soon admits that she has absolute power over him, and he asks to serve her in order that his happiness be complete. Sophonisbe asks only that he never send her to Rome as a slave, he consents, and they go off to be married that very night.

With the arrival of Scipion, the Roman general, an obstruction to the happiness of the newly joined couple is presented. The Romans insist that Sophonisbe is rightly part and parcel of the victory spoils and that she must be sent to Rome. Not only has Massinisse tainted his personal honor by marrying the widow of his greatest enemy, but he has overstepped the bounds of one dependent on Rome. Scipion also expresses the fear that Sophonisbe, who is known to hate the Roman empire, will exercise her influence on Massinisse and cause him, as she did Syphax, to abandon Rome.

Massinisse, alone, accuses the gods of giving no pleasure without pain. Confronted by the power of Rome, he also wonders where lies his own power. Rome is "a monster constantly reborn, a proud Harpy" (V. 1. 1412–13), and he is powerless. By his own death he will serve as an example of Rome's tyrannical authority. Momentarily agreeing to Scipion's demands in order to gain time, Massinisse plans his death. He sends Sophonisbe a cup of poison, which she drinks in the following scene, and, as the curtain falls and Massinisse gazes on her dead body, he pulls out a dagger with which to kill himself.

The story of the historic Sophonisbe and Massinisse is found in the works of Livy and Appien of Alexandria. Livy's version concentrates on the historic and political matters, and generally served authors who treated the story. Mairet, however, made more use of the account found in the *Histoires*, book 8 on the Punic Wars, by Appien.[8] Appien adds a certain amount of past information on the unfortunate couple. He writes that Sophonisbe and Massinisse had previously known each other in Carthage and had been engaged by her father Asdrubal. During Massinisse's absence, the Carthaginian senate forced Asdrubal to give his daughter to Syphax in order to appease him. Syphax, king of Numidia, had been plundering the territory of Carthage, and the marriage was an effective means of ensuring peace between the two kingdoms. This information proved valuable to Mairet in his version of the story.

The use of Massinisse and Sophonisbe as tragic hero and heroine was not without literary precedents.[9] One of the first dramatic adaptations was that of Trissino, who wrote his *Sofonisba* in 1515. It had been translated into French and was the prime influence on Mairet's rendering of the story. French versions of the same incidents include a translation by Mellin de Saint-Gelais (1559) and adaptations by Montchrestien (1596) and Nicolas de Montreux (1610), who used the anagrammatic pseudonym Olénix du Mont-Sacré. They were of little consequence for Mairet's handling of the text. After Mairet, two no less celebrated authors than Corneille and Voltaire produced their own versions of the events. In the preface to Corneille's *Sophonisbe* (1663), the author admits that the enormous and lasting success of Mairet's play makes his undertaking somewhat foolhardy.[10]

The changes which Mairet made in the historical facts of the Sophonisbe-Massinisse story show an important concern for the proprieties. Earlier treatments, which followed the events as recorded by history, created situations which would have proved unacceptable to Mairet's audience. For this reason he tailored the story to satisfy the moral demands of his own times. The principal problem lay in the fact that Sophonisbe's marriage to Massinisse made her bigamous, since Syphax was still alive. Mairet's decision to have the old king slain in battle alleviates that inconvenience by making the queen a widow.

Another major modification reflects an aesthetic consideration. The true Massinisse lived long after his wife's suicide. Mairet found that incompatible both with his conception of the tragic hero and his belief about the character of the tragic ending. "I have Massinisse do what he should have done," Mairet wrote in the preface of the play.[11] It was unreasonable to present a hero who continued to live after the person whom he loves has died, essentially by the hero's own hands. Mairet's conclusion is more tragic, more believable given the character he has created, and finally more dramatic.

In accommodating his tragedy to the twenty-four-hour rule Mairet gives further proof of his dramatic sense. Lest the love of Massinisse for Sophonisbe and their marriage appear a hastily concluded and unbelievable affair, the author has skillfully prepared the way. The Numidian prince is said to be of the African race most noted for sudden and ardent sentiments which demand equal passion in return. In addition, the rush of time is noted on several occasions. Massinisse himself explains that he hurried to marry Sophonisbe in the hope that upon arriving at court the Romans would accept their marriage as an accomplished fact, rather than forbidding it. In explaining Sophonisbe's passion Mairet makes use of the background information provided by Appien. At the time she was betrothed to Massinisse she fell in love with him, although he never had a chance to see her, according to the author. Time would have cured her, she says, had she not recently seen him on the field of battle. Upon viewing him with his visor up her old passion was reborn. Thus, as Mairet has conceived them and because of the pressure of the situation, both characters can give way immediately to their emotions. The short time span of the play, rather than constricting the action, serves to intensify it and to underline the fleeting quality of the characters' happiness. In this manner the unity of time is of dramatic utility to the tragedy.

The character of the play as a sudden and violent crisis is

further reinforced by unity of action. There is only one plot line—the consummation of the love of Sophonisbe and Massinisse, which the Romans forbid. The characters are few in number, and those principally concerned have a confidant or a friend to whom they can express their deepest sentiments. The play is tightly constructed, with monologues, dialogues, and scenes of confrontation, all of which add necessary information to the story or deepen our understanding of the characters, their motivation, and their reactions to the situation. The unity of place also adds to the concentration of interest, as the play takes place within, and immediately outside, the palace.

When one compares *Sophonisbe* to Mairet's preceding play *Virginie,* one is struck by the ease with which the tragedy conforms to the structure necessitated by application of the unities. *Virginie* suffered because of the rules. The tragicomedy appears unrealistic in its time conception, much as did *Le Cid,* in 1637, according to the critics. The play's story and respect of the unities simply do not coincide. In the case of *Sophonisbe* it is the perfect joining of character, plot, and unified structure that make of the tragedy one of the most important and influential plays of the preclassical era.

At the base of the dramatic structure of *Sophonisbe* is an aspect heretofore unimportant in Mairet's theater—political considerations. The plot conflict of the play, indeed of all three of the author's tragedies, results from a political confrontation. The characters are in part defined by their political beliefs but more properly by their reactions to higher authority.

As the play is enacted against the background of war and conquest, the characters are highly conscious of the tense situation and make constant reference to it. Sophonisbe's fear of enslavement by Rome and her proclaimed patriotism for Carthage find expression as the direct result of the imminent danger, and then the reality, of a Roman victory. Massinisse's tirades against the heavy burden of unjust authority arise because Scipion, as the representative of Rome, feels it necessary for the political good to separate him from the queen. The political conflict, while not resulting in battling armies on stage, determines to a great extent the mental state of the characters and provides motivation for their words and actions.

The Tragedies

Despite the political basis from which the play moves, it cannot be called a political tragedy as such, for the characters do not clash because they espouse different doctrines. Nor is the downfall of hero and heroine due primarily to their allegiance to a foreign power. The conflict arises because certain individuals hold to a higher value than obedience to political authority. That value is their love. The tragic lovers refuse to admit supremacy of political authority as it conflicts with their desire to accomplish their union, and they grant primacy instead to their love. They act directly against the higher power by refusing to follow its orders, thereby bringing about the conflict situation.

The characters thus in part define themselves by their response to the following question: to whom or what does an individual owe final obedience? Such characters as Scipion and Lélie argue that duty to the state stands first in order of importance. Opposing them, the lovers attempt to establish that love must be placed above all other considerations, even political ones. The conflict is love versus the exercise of authority and obedience to political orders.

The use of the political theme and the resulting conflict of authority can be considered a variation on structures which Mairet had previously employed. The conflict of parental authority, seen in *Sylvie* and *Silvanire*, presents the same pattern of one group insisting on its unqualified right to determine the lives of others. Fossinde's highly charged criticism of the conduct of Sylvie's father is paralleled in Massinisse's outbursts against Rome. The same cautions against too strong a show of force on the part of authority arise in the tragedy and in the earlier plays. The role of the heroine's mother in *Sylvie* and *Silvanire* is primarily to interject a note of sympathetic understanding and to plead for a more humane course of action. In a similar manner, Lélie, Scipion's lieutenant, warns against harsh handling of the delicate situation. The dialogue between Scipion and Lélie, the former advocating force, the latter cautioning against it, is a repeat of the discussion between the king and his counselor in *Chryséide* and a similar scene in *Sylvie*.[12] These established patterns of authority do not collapse or even weaken during the course of the earlier plays. The happy endings of the first three plays come about because of an appeal to higher authority or because of the intervention of some greater power, usually from the religious realm. The tragic ending of *Sophonisbe* results from the absence of any power greater than political authority. In this respect the political basis of the tragedy seems to combine the structure of the parental or social conflict and the ultimate deciding power given to religion and to the gods. Just as the individual in the pastoral tragicomedies is helpless against the will of the gods, so in the tragedies he is helpless against the power of political authority. The conflict based on political power is the juncture of two earlier structural patterns, both familiar to the author, indeed both commonplace in plays of the times. Mairet's accomplishment is that he molded them into the tragic framework.

Comparison of the tragedy to the structural patterns of the earlier plays can be carried one step further in discussing *Sophonisbe*. We have said that the characters of the pastoral tragicomedy formed two well-defined separate groups and that interaction between the two groups or ties from one to the other were considered, in a very loose understanding of the word, a crime. In the tragedy the characters likewise form two distinct groups but by political rather than social definition. They are enemies separated by hatred and by war. In the strictest sense of the term contact with a member of the opposing side is a crime. So Syphax criticizes Sophonisbe, and Scipion Massinisse. In the tragedy it is precisely a break in the fixed order which creates the conflict situation. The hero ties himself to a woman who represents the defeated enemy of Rome, one who hates the empire, and he refuses to renounce his love for her. The crime is love of the enemy.

Charged by those in authority with crimes against their countries, their leaders, their allies, and more importantly against their personal virtues and honor, the hero and heroine offer little justification. The full realization of the magnitude of an ultimately indefensible position removes all possiblity of self-defense. The only reason given is love. The power of love, effacing reasons of patriotism, respect, and glory, possesses the lovers to the extent that they are incapable of viewing a situation except through the eyes of their passion. Their identification with the emotion even goes so far as to present an excuse for their recognized crimes. Massinisse speaks of the supreme power of love which both caused his error and excuses it.

Scipion and Lélie, the Roman military leaders, do not take such a view of the lovers' state. They emphasize everything which Massinisse has dismissed in his arguments in favor of love. To Scipion the hero is merely a "poor blinded spirit" who does not recognize his seduction by the false charms of love. The prince has lost all reasoning power and judgment. He has foregone honor and renounced life as it is motivated by noble actions. The two sets of characters participate in two separate fields of reality—political expediency based on a real situation of large-scale importance, and individual, personal happiness founded on a shared emotion in the simple context of the couple.

The individuals caught in the conflict between their understanding of political forces and their desire for personal fulfillment do not automatically choose to honor love at all cost. Mairet portrays psychological conflicts within certain characters as the realization of their almost impossible position dawns on them. Through the presentation of dilemmas at the individual level the author succeeds in creating more complete human characters. Sophonisbe, the tragic queen, is entirely possessed by love for Massinisse, but she fully realizes the consequences of her situation. Trapped between love of country and love of her country's enemy she struggles to right her sense of values, and her lucidity heightens the tragic split in her desire. She dare not pray for Massinisse's victory; she cannot pray for Massinisse's defeat. Motivated by love and conflicting patriotism, Sophonisbe knows full well the outcome of the dilemma. Although she "burns with desire to preserve [her] glory at the expense of [her] life" (II. 1. 363–64), Sophonisbe is reduced to following the admonitions of the fury which the god (love) orders up in her. Her protests and fears are in vain, for she will be led by love.

Part of the queen's dilemma resides in the uncertainty of her emotional state. At that point in the play Massinisse neither loves her nor knows that she loves him. With the resolution of the problem and their marriage before act III, the burden of ensuring their future happiness falls to Massinisse. The major interest of the play shifts from the queen to him, as does the personal-political conflict, for the outcome of his conversations with Scipion will determine both his destiny and that of his new wife.

The crime of which Syphax accused Sophonisbe in the opening scene of the play, ingratitude, is repeated and strengthened as Scipion criticizes Massinisse. Just as the old king had ensured his wife's happiness and well-being, the power of Rome decided the Numidian prince's victory. In refusing to relinquish Sophonisbe as a rightful trophy of the Roman victory, Massinisse proves himself ungrateful for their aid and unworthy of further support. Furthermore, Scipion insists that he is abandoning the very quality which won him his throne—the life of an active hero. According to the Roman general, the life that Massinisse presently envisions for himself is the very opposite of what he should be striving for. Like Sophonisbe in her self-accusations, Massinisse as seen by Scipion is renouncing his very being as a hero, a person worthy of glory. The crime in the eyes of Rome is not merely political, although that consideration is paramount. Massinisse's decision to marry Sophonisbe represents a renunciation of the values that have created the Roman empire. The crime against the empire is heinous, but the crime against oneself and consequently against heroism is far worse.

Mairet's characterization of the Romans is skillful. Scipion is the older military leader who believes that only a strong hand will bring the prince back to his right mind. Lélie, his lieutenant and probably closer to the age of the hero, cautions against such a show of blatant force. He believes that the prince is not yet lost and can still be convinced of the rightness and necessity of abandoning Sophonisbe. Both Romans agree, however, on the principal issue—that individual sentiment must be stifled and that political expediency should rule one's actions. There can be no individual right when it counters the best concerns of the country. Love is termed "fatal," a "blind fury," and it is claimed that love leads to shame.

Cast against the formidable power of political authority, the individual asks in vain that he be allowed to make his own decision regarding his fate and that this decision be honored by those in authority. The loss of this basic right results in a denial of the characters' humanity and places them in a state of unacceptable subservience. Massinisse's problem is that he fully realizes his personal debt to Rome, as did Sophonisbe hers to Syphax, and he also recognizes the reasoning behind Scipion's demands. After assuring Scipion that the queen would never draw him away from his friendship with Rome, he asks that she be given to him as recompense for his service to the empire. When Scipion refuses, Massinisse explodes in fury at his helplessness against the power of Roman authority, giving testimony to the futile position of the individual attempting to bend the state's will to his own wishes. Finally resigning himself to the situation, Massinisse pronounces the line which symbolizes the power of the state, its injustice, and the helplessness of the individual. "Il faut bien le vouloir quand Rome l'a voulu" ("One must want [accept] it when Rome wants [has decided] it.") (V. 2. 1541).

The situation of the hero and heroine is tragic, because their love is not allowed to exist in a world involved in political strife and governed by political considerations without recourse to a higher, possibly more just authority. The union of the lovers is a crime, because through it they transcend barriers considered absolutes by the other characters. Love itself might possibly be acceptable, but when the problem is compounded by the fact that two supposed enemies are joined in love, there can be no solution except an end, forcible or otherwise, to their union. Rather than renounce their love in order to live, the tragic lovers glorify it in death. The tragedy arises because this ending is inevitable, the only possible solution given their situation. The suicides of Sophonisbe and Massinisse represent for them the only means of avoiding dishonor by acquiescing to the Roman demands, and of preserving some measure of personal dignity and glory. Sophonisbe's resolve to die is strengthened by the realization that her death will not only spare her from slavery, but establish her glory as an individual who was feared by the greatest of empires.

Sophonisbe stands at the midpoint in Mairet's career and marks the culmination of his previous dramatic efforts. All of the author's talents appear to their best advantage in the tragedy. His power of creating human characters succeeds admirably in the portrait of Syphax, the embittered and jealous old man; Massinisse, the glorious hero and ardent lover; Scipion and Lélie, soldiers devoted to duty and the cause of Rome; and Sophonisbe, the heroine. All are believable characterizations, and show the author's fine psychological understanding in their reactions to the tense situation. The story itself is unencumbered by excessive detail and action. Its sobriety, especially in comparison with the author's preceding works, is of course the very element which makes possible the application of the rules. For that reason, the unities finally find a play which displays them in the best light, as they become an integral part of the work rather than an unaccommodating and ill-fitting frame.

Despite the fact that Mairet's *Sophonisbe* has been called the first regular French tragedy, such is not precisely the case. Théophile's *Pyrame et Thisbé* followed the rules with sufficient faithfulness to merit the appellation, although its regular form did not prove to be influential. Rotrou's tragedy *Hercule Mourant* (1634), which preceded *Sophonisbe* by a short period of time, conformed to the unities in much the same manner as Mairet's *Silvanire*. The importance of Mairet's tragedy lies not primarily in the realm of rules but rather in that of influence. With *Sophonisbe* was born, suddenly and unexpectedly, a rekindling of interest in the dormant genre of the regular historical tragedy. The success of the play resulted in a sudden proliferation of tragedies on the French stage, fourteen in the year 1635–36 alone.[13] Not without interest is the fact that *Sophonisbe* was the first French tragedy based on Roman history since Hardy's *Coriolan*. The dramatist's choice of source material proved an essential factor in the orientation of tragedy in years to come. Furthermore, the play's concentration on a psychological crisis and a small number of characters dictated both dramatic form and content for the authors who followed Mairet. Even more than respect of the unities, the violent, intense conflict within the souls of the characters must be seen as an influential contribution to the genre.[14] Ensconced in the framework dictated by the unities, *Sophonisbe* depicted the type of situation most consistent and most compatible with that form.

The Tragedies

It is this dramatic juncture of subject and form which proves Mairet's greatest legacy to French tragedy.

III Marc Antoine

Mairet's *Marc Antoine*[15] follows his success with *Sophonisbe* in presenting a tragedy based on an episode from Roman history. Both tragedies center around a political conflict, a war between Rome and an African power. The hero in both plays sides not with the forces of his own nationality but with those that combat them—Massinisse with the Romans, Antony with the Egyptians. The confrontation results in a Roman triumph, which brings about the death of hero and heroine. Against this background of political conflict moves a drama of impossible love.

At the beginning of the play the audience sees Marc Antony speaking to his troops prior to their final battle with Octavius Caesar. He encourages them to continue their valorous deeds and assures them that good fortune will bring about their triumph. In private, Antony admits to having little faith in the soldiers' courage and fidelity. He must flatter them, even though they may prove unworthy of his confidence to the point of abandoning their leader if the battle should prove difficult. The scene changes to the palace, and Cleopatra enters. She expresses vague, undefinable fears about her present situation. In order to test her, Antony announces that the most recent encounter with the enemy troops has ended in a defeat. Cleopatra replies that no battle can be lost since he still lives and loves her. In reality Antony was victorious, and Cleopatra had previously been told so. The act concludes with Antony's declarations of love.

The hero's fears mount as he learns of the defection of one soldier who had been given golden arms by Cleopatra in recognition of his past service. But he sees no other option than to entrust his fate to the troops in the forthcoming battle. His lieutenant Lucile has another plan. He has had Octavia, Antony's wife and Octavius's sister, come to Egypt from Rome. Their admitted purpose is to see if she can persuade Antony to accept her help and leave Cleopatra. Momentarily left alone as Lucile goes to get Octavia, the hero is filled with shame and remorse at having so cowardly rejected his wife. She enters, and despite her touching avowal of continued patience and her pleas that he follow Caesar's example in fleeing the Egyptian queen, Octavia does not succeed in shaking Antony's intent. He must stay in Egypt, fight Octavius's troops and remain faithful to Cleopatra. Their love, he says, makes them inseparable. Faithful to the end, Octavia promises to help her husband in any way she can. The famous battle then takes place in the interval between the second and third acts.

As the third act begins, the high priest tells of signs and portents of impending danger. He believes that the gods are jealous of their authority, which Cleopatra has usurped. She has dared dress herself as Isis and has named her children the Sun and the Moon. Such extravagance can only bring about her downfall. The queen arrives, petrified with fear and dread, and learns of Antony's defeat. His soldiers simply capitulated before the oncoming troops. Antony himself believes the defeat due to Cleopatra's betrayal of him to Octavius. She tries to flee, but he catches her and vents his fury. He reproaches the queen for her ingratitude, accusing her of being the cause of all his misfortune. Cleopatra refuses to defend herself, since she can do nothing to convince Antony of her innocence.

At the beginning of the fourth act, Lucile promises to give all possible aid to Antony, but the hero sees death as the only solution to his desperate situation. When Iras announces Cleopatra's suicide, the hero's resolution to die is strengthened. He must follow her in death. Presenting his sword Antony asks Lucile as his only remaining friend to kill him. Instead Lucile chooses to kill himself. Marveling at his friend's courage and virtue, Antony takes the sword and stabs himself as well. Iras returns to find Antony wounded. She tells him that the news of the queen's death was only a story designed to test his love. He asks to be taken to her and dies in Cleopatra's arms content to know her innocence. Shortly after the hero's death Proclée, one of Octavius's lieutenants, enters and prevents Cleopatra from committing suicide. He begs her to live so that Octavius may exercise his goodness in pardoning her. Octavius himself comes to console her and to promise clemency, although he

The Tragedies

should punish her, since her power and ambition have favored an enemy of Rome. She argues that she did not act from personal ambition, but from faithfulness to her husband. Octavius enjoins her to live, and, feigning acquiescence, she agrees. In reality her decision to join Antony in death does not weaken, but she feels it necessary to play for time. When finally left alone, she commands her servants to bring the vase of serpents. Octavius's false promises do not blind her to her duty to Antony. As an example of constancy and love, she chooses death and has the snakes bite her arm. The two handmaidens follow her example and then lead the queen to her nearby chambers. Learning of her suicide, Octavius pronounces Cleopatra worthy of the kings from whom she is descended.

Although the relationship between hero, heroine, and Rome shows basic similarities to the plot of *Sophonisbe*, there are important differences between the two tragedies. In *Marc Antoine* Rome appears to play the role of protagonist and receives some criticism from the hero and heroine, but political authority as such is not the question. *Marc Antoine* is much less politically oriented than the earlier tragedy. In *Sophonisbe* the Romans' victory and their subsequent power over Massinisse as their ally and the queen as the defeated enemy provided the barrier to the hero's love for the heroine, specifically in the person of the Roman general Scipion. In *Marc Antoine* no one character fulfills that primarily political role. Rather it is Antony's own position of defeated hero that renders further happiness with Cleopatra impossible. Rome stands at one remove from the crucial issue, causing his defeat and only indirectly preventing his continued union with the queen. The personal and political levels of the play do not intertwine so neatly as in *Sophonisbe*. The political element functions merely as the background for an essentially personal tragedy. A brief examination of the two heroines' attitudes toward the reigning political power shows the second tragedy's insistence on the personal sphere of action.

The position of the individual in regard to the political situation in both tragedies becomes that of a simple pawn, an element of political expediency. To the conquering troops the heroine represents merely a war trophy to be seized and displayed as proof of victory. The attitudes of the two heroines, however, toward the possibility of capture and eventual enslavement in Rome show the important distinction between them, emphasizing the shift to the purely personal. Sophonisbe can imagine no conditions under which she would serve as a slave in Rome. Led by her avid patriotism and her equally intense hatred of servitude, she would rather die than have Carthage dishonored in her person. This belief predates her love for Massinisse. Cleopatra announces that she would willingly accept being a slave if Antony remained with her. Patriotism, of no little importance in forming the character of the earlier heroine, provides no character motivation in *Marc Antoine*. No passionate lines of love for Egypt spring from the queen's mouth, no ringing condemnation of a less glorious life than that of a ruling monarch.

The suicide of the Carthaginian queen seems both a political and a personal maneuver. She kills herself in order to avoid discrediting her royal blood and her native land. Sophonisbe, the more complex of the two heroines, presents a combination of motivations: her pride, her patriotism, as well as her love for Massinisse. Though Cleopatra is no less proud or courageous than Sophonisbe, her decision to seek in death an end to her torment arises solely from her desire to remain faithful to Antony. Cleopatra functions on one level alone and draws her character from her love of the hero. Should that love subsist, she could accept anything. The Romans interpret this attitude as a weakness, and Octavius does not believe a woman capable of an honorable suicide. When reminded that Sophonisbe succeeded in a similar undertaking, he merely answers that all women do not have the courage of the daughter of Asdrubal.

The tragedy also presents the crime of Antony at the personal level, emphasizing not his revolt against Rome but his abandonment and divorce of his lawful wife, Octavia, in order to marry Cleopatra. The Romans term him *ingrat*, a word which must be taken to mean faithless, inconstant, and unvirtuous. In marrying Cleopatra, according to the Romans, Antony sacrificed both duty to Rome and duty to wife. Unlike Massinisse, however, Antony never finds himself in the position of having to make a choice between duty to country and fidelity to his love. He no longer recognizes Rome as a viable authority with power over him. In renouncing Octavia he symbolically severed all ties with Rome. Choosing to remain with Cleopatra he takes the path which, he believes, will ensure both his personal honor and his love for Cleopatra. The primary criticism directed by the Romans against Massinisse, that he had abandoned active heroism, does not apply in the case of Antony. He constantly tries to reestablish his position as the heroic victor.

There exists another key to the character of Cleopatra which deserves discussion. It is fatalism, which forms a leitmotif throughout the play. In expressing her fears early in the first act, she says that she and Antony were born to cause each other's misfortune. They must follow their inevitable destiny rather than flee it. The foreboding atmosphere is similar to that found in Mairet's earliest plays. Unlike the pastoral tragicomedies, however, the tragedy avoids the overly vocal despair that marked the pastoral heroes. The characters accept the situation, neither questioning nor criticizing it. They acknowledge this sense of man's dependence on some unknown higher power, although man's lower position is not of essential dramatic importance to the play.

Mentions of dreams and omens serve to create a generally fatalistic climate, but the specific danger belongs to a different concern. The inevitability of the tragedy stems from individual helplessness in regard to a concrete situation, rather than from metaphysical despair in confrontation with the supernatural powers. The characters do not indulge in lamentations about the injustices of fate or the gods. Even Cleopatra, the one who most clearly views herself as destroyed by destiny, does not complain about the human position. The heroes and heroines of the tragedies more frequently express despair about their present situation in regard to a force directed against them from the real world, such as political authority, attacking armies, or individual helplessness in the face of such foes.

The gods are mentioned in several scenes of *Marc Antoine*, and their attitude toward men shows similarities to that expressed in *Sophonisbe*. The heroine of the first tragedy believed that she had been too happy to please the gods. Massinisse also mentions that the gods customarily cause sweetness to be followed by bitterness, that human happiness makes them envious, and that they mix sorrow with pleasure for fear that earthly joy might resemble their own, which is perfect.[16] The gods in *Marc Antoine* are jealous of their authority, according to the high priest Aristée. Cleopatra has committed sacrilegious improprieties, and the vengeance of the gods will fall on her. Although the priest speaks of "divine anger" and the "insolent fury of fate," this theme does not reach a level of great importance. The characters never draw any moral lesson from their suffering. The religious issue of crimes against the gods and heavenly vengeance remains an undercurrent, a given and accepted situation, and does not provide the basis of the play.

The play's primary theme continues the discussion in *Sophonisbe* of supposed crimes committed by hero and heroine against heroic virtue, and their defense of such crimes. Mairet's first tragedy placed the hero in the position of having to choose between acceptance of political authority, thereby denying his love, and rejection of acknowledged duty in favor of personal emotions. In *Sophonisbe* the hero could not avoid committing some crime. His priorities determined that it be the conscious repudiation of duty to political leaders. Massinisse's dilemma showed the tragic juncture between two domains, private sentiment and public authority, as they sought to rule his life. *Marc Antoine* lacks the dramatic impact of the earlier hero's impossible situation by avoiding presentation of any true dilemma, either external or personal. The tragedy concentrates on one issue, the victory of constancy over infidelity.

In general it can be said that heroic characters owe allegiance to four separate realms—to their gods, to their country and its leaders, to the person they love, and to themselves. The heroic virtues then grow from established and repeated proofs of fidelity in all four areas. As defined by the characters who oppose them, the lovers in Mairet's tragedies are guilty of ignoring or rejecting necessary ties to all realms except honor to the loved one. Constancy to the lover stands as the sole remaining heroic virtue. In fact, the desire to prove faithful in this one area overpowers adherence to all others, destroying their significance for the lovers as they struggle to force acceptance of their union and to preserve it. Constancy alone creates their heroism. The lovers' faith in each other, in their love, and in its reality provides the heroic strength needed to overcome their impossible situation and eventually to face death.

In the first scene of *Sophonisbe* Syphax's accusations of the young queen provide the double thrust of the crime of faithlessness for that tragedy—marital infidelity and betrayal of country. Mairet puts aside the second meaning in *Marc Antoine,* concentrating instead on various ramifications of faithfulness to one's partner. He broadens the term to include friendship and devotion of soldiers to their leader as well as marital constancy.

As examples of the constant recurrence of the theme, Antony accuses Caesar of ingratitude for earlier assistance in his victories. He fears the less than noble character of his soldiers. The hero accuses himself of the crime when confronted by the faithful Octavia. In abandoning her he acted in a less than fully virtuous manner. Mairet's addition of Antony's first wife to the story illustrates his concern with the theme of fidelity. Octavia's appearance underlines her own persistent constancy, Antony's crimes against her, as well as his insistence that he must remain faithful to Cleopatra because he loves her. The final element, love, explains why Antony cannot reject the Egyptian queen and return to Octavia. Fidelity founded upon a mutually shared sentiment, the love of Antony and Cleopatra in this case, presents the overriding motivation for the hero's actions.

Cleopatra most fully represents this theme. Mairet does not portray her as an ambitious, glory-seeking, selfish queen, the characterization most commonly associated with her. Despite the fact that Octavia is Antony's first lawful wife, Mairet has Cleopatra make the most moving defense of marital fidelity and constancy in love. Criticized by Octavius in the final act for having favored the ambition of an enemy of the Roman people and Senate, she responds that "the faith that Marriage demands of us" dictated her actions. Abandoning her husband, even in order to restore her own political power, would be a shameful and odious sin. She argues further that fidelity is no crime. She willingly accepts death, thereby reuniting herself with Antony. In such scenes the character of Cleopatra shows strikingly well the strength of enduring constancy and the depths of courage that love can create.

Defense of love and of faithfulness provides the play's most moving moments but does not succeed in making of the tragedy a play equal to *Sophonisbe* in either interest or intensity. Compared to Mairet's first tragedy, *Marc Antoine* seems a step backward in his career. Because of the lack of either a well-defined personal conflict or a confrontation between opposing forces on stage, the second tragedy does not have the power of the first. The characters, though skillfully delineated, never achieve the dramatic interaction necessary for the success of any theatrical endeavor. Many scenes appear to be simultaneous monologues rather than dialogues, as each person carefully speaks his piece, independent and mindless of the others. Each individual character possesses his own motivating factor, Cleopatra's love and fidelity, Antony's desire to reestablish himself as a hero and to remain with Cleopatra, Octavia's persistence in recapturing Antony, Octavius's wish to preserve Cleopatra as a victory trophy. Their paths cross only haphazardly, never fusing into dramatic action as do those of Sophonisbe, Massinisse, and Scipion. Mairet likewise overuses lengthy speeches. Octavia delivers one speech of 119 verses (act II, scene 3), and Antony has one almost 80 lines long (III, 4). These overlong declamations typify the tragedy's general lack of action. A strong scene between the two lovers would go far toward remedying the situation, but of their three scenes (I, 3; III, 4; and V, 1) none reaches any level of dramatic intensity. Mairet has unfortunately not found the right combination of character, plot, and dramatic interest to create another *Sophonisbe*.

IV Le grand et dernier Solyman

Le grand et dernier Solyman ou la Mort de Mustapha[17] was one of two plays directly inspired by the Italian Prospero Bonarelli's *Solimano* and presented at the same time on the two Parisian stages. The Hôtel de Bourgogne staged Mairet's

The Tragedies

tragedy, while the Théâtre du Marais acted the rival Dalibray's *Soliman,* a tragicomedy.[18] Mairet thus found himself a second time in direct competition for audience interest and patronage. It is unfortunately impossible to ascertain which play garnered the greater success.

A political conflict again serves as the background for the tragedy. The war between Thrace and Persia is essentially decided before the play opens, but the Persians refuse to acknowledge defeat. Solyman, sultan of Thrace, orders preparations for one final encounter in order to convince the enemy of its inevitable destruction. Soon, however, a court intrigue takes over as the characters' primary interest, and they forget plans for the battle. Nonetheless, the background of two nations at war remains a necessary element of the play's atmosphere of suspicion and fear. Through a twist of fate in the final scenes, political considerations return to support the claims of court intriguers, and concern for the good of the state finally forces the tragic outcome.

The first act opens with two exposition scenes, one for each of the two plot lines which soon converge. Roxelane, the sultaness, explains to a slave girl her fear of the sultan's son Mustapha. She and another of Solyman's wives both gave birth to sons some twenty years ago at a one-day interval. As the elder, the other son would have killed Roxelane's son upon becoming sultan, in order to cease any ambitious plotting. To avoid his eventual murder, Roxelane had her son hidden by a slave and put a dead child in its place. Since that time she has had no news of her own son, whom she calls Sélim. The second scene introduces Despine, a Persian princess disguised as a man, who is supposedly spying on the enemy encampments. In reality, she and Mustapha have been in love since the time the Persians held him prisoner during the wars two years ago. She is seeking some means of meeting him to renew their vows to each other. Her governor Alvante reacts strongly against such a betrayal of both her country and her royal blood. He agrees to aid her and takes from her two blank letters signed by her father, as her pledge to Mustapha. Mairet has thus carefully prepared the entrance of the hero, for the audience now knows the relationship of the two main female characters to him. He is hated by Roxelane, representing his home country, and loved by Despine, representing the enemy. This paradoxical position will result in Mustapha's downfall, as it caused that of Massinisse and Antony.

An intrigue led by Rustan, a disgruntled courtier, soon becomes the play's principal interest. Mustapha's growing glory and esteem have thwarted Rustan's own ambitious desires. In order to supplant him Rustan conceives a plot which will discredit Mustapha in the eyes of his father. The sultaness represents the key element of his plan, as Rustan will play on her own fears and draw her into his circle of influence. Fortuitously, Osman, Rustan's confidant, finds the letters which Alvante has thrown away in a fit of anger, refusing to act in Despine's scheme.

The complications of the conspiracy are multiplied in the second act. Rustan skillfully makes the sultaness fear for her life as a pawn in Mustapha's quest for power. A credulous, superstitious woman, she believes him, and in court she expresses to the sultan her fears for his life as well. Acmat alone tries to defend the prince, but Rustan destroys the calming effect of the former's words by producing forged letters implicating Mustapha in a Persian plot to murder the sultan.

Alvante also indulges in deceit. He tells Despine that Mustapha has rejected her plea and publicly mocked her shameless impudence. Fully aware of the audacity of her desire to see him, she blames only herself but calls for vengeance or death to still her fury.

Mustapha receives several warnings about Rustan's treachery from those still faithful to him in the court, as well as from Bajazet, his lieutenant and friend. The prince refuses to flee, seeing that alternative as an admission of guilt, but he is also unwilling to defend himself actively, preferring to leave his defense to a righteous heaven. Bajazet argues that heaven demands that we protect ourselves against earthly schemes, but he cannot persuade the prince to act in his own behalf. As a page announces an uprising in the army, Mustapha goes to quell it.

The sultan and sultaness are by now totally in Rustan's power and convinced of the imminent danger that Mustapha repre-

The Tragedies 123

sents. Although Solyman's paternal love fights the belief in his son's guilt, he feels powerless in face of the situation. A palace guard forces Despine into the court after arresting her. Her admission that she is a Persian spy serves to increase the royal couple's fears. Later her path crosses that of Mustapha as Rustan leads her to prison. She calls him cruel and ungrateful. Rustan steps in to prevent the prince from taking Despine away, and in anger Bajazet mortally wounds the conspirator. Mustapha sees in that violent act the beginning of a reign of terror which will include his own death.

The sultan allows his son a final interview with Despine. The young people pass from accusations of treachery and pleas of innocence to admission of love, as Alvante admits his seemingly harmless trick. Believing that the gods were against the union of Despine and Mustapha, he refused to serve his young mistress and took it upon himself to thwart her plans. Their sorrow becomes joy when Solyman announces his intention to join them in the closest possible bond. He gives as his motivation the good of the state. Mustapha soon notices that his father's face belies his words, and he perceives a possible double meaning in the sultan's promises. Despine tries to dissuade him from such pessimism, when Solyman's meaning suddenly becomes clear. A page gives them a package containing, he says, material to explain the sultan's intention. Uncovering it the lovers find an ax and linen cloths to bind them. Rather than dishonor themselves in futile resistance Mustapha and Despine decide to face death knowing their own virtue and constancy. The guards lead them off to be executed.

Roxelane learns of her error when an old slave tells about an oracle predicting that she would be the cause of her son's death. Through the intervention of an old peasant woman, the entire story is made known. The son of Circasse, the other sultaness, died at birth, and she ordered that a live infant be found to replace it. The child whom her servants eventually brought to her was Roxelane's son. He, of course, had been left with the peasant woman immediately beforehand. Unable to bear the thought of killing her own son the sultaness commits suicide. Solyman, learning of his son's complete innocence by Roxelane's death and Rustan's deathbed confession, vows to finish his days in perpetual mourning. As the play ends, Bajazet and the soldiers storm into the palace pledging to kill both the innocent and the guilty in a purge of vengeance for the death of Mustapha.

All the themes discussed in treating Mairet's earlier tragedies recur in *Solyman*. The political climate provides an initial impetus for the drama as it places the hero and heroine in opposing camps. Mistrust of them automatically results from their diverging national allegiance. The opposition to them comes at least in part from the reigning authority. In the face of such a barrier they find in their faith in each other the strength to face death. Love between enemies, opposition from political authority, constancy when confronted with certain death—such earlier themes find echoes in *Solyman*. The major emphasis is not, however, on the young lovers, but on Solyman, the leader who orders their death. Despine and Mustapha could almost be called minor figures in the drama. Their principal role is to bring about the situation which causes great torment in the mind of Solyman. One initial weakness becomes immediately clear. Although Mairet obviously means Solyman to be the major character, he has not drawn the sultan with sufficient force or endowed him with an adequate characterization to incite audience sympathy. On the other hand, the two young lovers are almost too well drawn, for Mairet has created fully rounded roles which attract attention to them. After their deaths the audience has little desire to learn of Solyman's fate.

Convinced of his son's collusion with the enemy, Solyman must protect both the country and himself as its leader. His personal sentiments, love for his son, all but render impossible the act which the good of the state seems to demand. Caught between political duty and paternal love, he lives a dilemma not unlike that of Massinisse. He defines his state as a search for himself with no possibility of truly finding himself within his own being. Consequently, as a lover who fears his partner's infidelity, Solyman loses his ability to make decisions and act upon them. Only at the prodding of Roxelane and Rustan does he move from his state of inaction and indecision. Believing that he is acting for his own good and for the good of the state, he orders the execution. The tragedy is that Solyman has put his trust in circumstantial evidence, superstition, and suspicion, for they combined to outweigh his personal feelings.

The key to Solyman's decision and to the general pattern of action throughout the play lies in Mairet's use of deception and artifice. To some extent one finds situations based on deceptive means present in all of Mairet's plays. At times they support the true conflict and at others they replace it, creating an artificial conflict which the characters take to be real. The use of deception runs from simple trickery, in order to discover the truth, to fraudulent perversion and suppression of the truth. In this respect *Marc Antoine* presents an interesting pattern of four separate incidents of deception, two of which are taken to be true, thereby resulting in the deaths of Marc Antony and Cleopatra. In order to test her love, Antony announces to Cleopatra (I. 4) that he has lost the battle. She knows otherwise and does not believe him; thus, no problem arises. In a mirroring scene (IV. 2) Cleopatra, testing Antony's affection, has Iras tell him of her suicide. Antony believes the news and kills himself. Feigning clemency while only desiring her as a trophy, Octavius asks the queen to live. She does not believe his offer of pardon but feigns agreement. He accepts her word as true, thereby allowing her the chance to kill herself. In both cases where characters accepted artifice as reality, death resulted. As Iras says upon finding Antony wounded, he "is truly dying because of a make-believe death" (IV. 3).

Artifice, lies, fraud, deception—the entire gamut of means of perverting the truth occur in *Solyman*. In the first five scenes of the play various characters reveal four separate past incidents founded on deception and disguise. Indeed, the course of the play runs from one deceitful act to another, as the truth is either wholly absent or totally disregarded, and every character becomes a victim of illusion masking reality. Only when the truth of the very first trick, the exchange of children, comes to light do the members of the sultan's court and the audience finally learn the truth. The one truthful element, that Mustapha loved the foreign princess, chanced to support the false claims of those plotting against him.

The progression from *Sophonisbe* to *Solyman* in use of deceptive means and dependence on artifice as plot indicates a loss of the feeling of human tragedy so powerful in the first play. Rather than being tragic, *Solyman* is melodramatic in its overuse of contrivance and irony. The deaths of Massinisse and Sophonisbe, and those of Antony and Cleopatra, result from a recognized real situation. The characters are humanly incapable of changing it or succeeding against it. Their outcome proves both inevitable and tragic. The element most lacking in *Solyman* is precisely that inevitability. Had Solyman received Rustan's letter, had Alvante not thrown away Despine's message, and had not just the right person been there at just the right time to pick it up, or had Roxelane learned earlier about the oracle and the true identity of her lost son the deaths would not have taken place. Whereas in the two earlier tragedies ruse and artifice were used in conjunction with the plot line while remaining subordinate to it, contrivance in *Solyman* has completely usurped the role of plot to the detrimental weakening of any truly tragic element. Artifice, the false conflict, has been invested with the role of the true conflict.

Before concluding the discussion of Mairet's final tragedy, the particular setting and atmosphere of *Solyman* call for some examination. Mairet presents a striking portrayal of an Oriental court as a place fraught with danger to the unwary, grounded in suspicion and paralyzed by fear. Such a portrayal is certainly in keeping with the preconceived notions that the audience of the time had about the infidels of the East. The innocent and the guilty alike suffer the consequences of the total disregard for truth, reason, or honesty. The world of the play seems bound on a self-destructive collision course. Given Mairet's less than fully cordial relationship with the powers of the French court it would be interesting to speculate that there existed some element of willed comparison between it and the court of Solyman. In dedicating the tragedy to the Duchesse de Montmorency seven years after her husband's execution, Mairet, undoubtedly referring to the Duke's death, states that the play is "of all my works the most likely to nourish your melancholy."[19] He goes on to say, "You will discover here [in the play] courtly intrigues and wickedness

The Tragedies

which will confirm the wise resolution that you have taken never again to set out on a Sea which gave proof of its own infidelity by such a pitiful shipwreck."[20] Mairet never forgave Richelieu his role in the death of the author's first protector, and on many occasions he pledged fidelity to the duke's memory. Therein lies the note of bitterness behind the author's portrayal of so despicable a court, although to state that overt criticism of the ruling powers is Mairet's principal objective in writing the play would most likely be an exaggeration. The dedication was written two years after the play's initial performances, and the comparison between the two courts could as easily have been an afterthought on the author's part.

In the dedication to *Solyman* Mairet professes that "the play is in all the rules of Tragedy." Indeed, it is difficult to fault the author's application of the three unities. The entire play takes place in the sultan's court or a short distance from its walls. Following the unity of time, the tragedy's action can be understood to take place within a period of twenty-four hours. For the unity of action, all events move toward the conclusion, the murder of the young hero and heroine with the resulting deaths which follow. Because of the contrived and gratuitous nature of so many of the play's events, however, *Solyman* does not succeed as a human tragedy. Perhaps the work represents a tragedy of errors or a tragedy of circumstantial evidence, but the important events are due to chance and fortuitous happenings rather than resulting from human desire, volition, or intention. The circumstances remove the action from the human realm, thereby sacrificing necessary integration of events and characters from which tragedy can grow. The only glimmer of true tragedy lies in the conflict between Solyman's love for his son and the weight of evidence against him. This does not save the play from being melodramatic rather than tragic. *Solyman* finally seems less mature than *Sophonisbe*, because Mairet has neglected the very element which makes his first tragedy a key word in the history of French theater—a psychological dilemma which results from the characters and their particular situation rather than being imposed on them by circumstance.

V *Pastoral and Tragedy*

Comparison of Mairet's first three dramatic works, written in the pastoral tragicomic vein, and his three tragedies shows a pattern of recurring themes and interests. Among them such aspects as love, the presence of a greater power as obstacle, strict divisions between groups of characters, and an often expressed religious belief in the goodness of the gods play roles of varying importance. Through differing emphases of these common aspects Mairet creates the contrasting worlds of the pastoral and the tragedy.

The portrayal of love does not differ significantly in the two groups of plays. Love is an inner fire, a passion born of a glance, to be cherished and honored above all else. It is innocent before marriage and constant afterward. The various terms used by the characters to personify love do not vary greatly from play to play. According to the attitude of the character love is a god, the master of fate, or a monster, a tyrant. Love is both the illness and the remedy. That which differentiates the treatment of love in the two dramatic worlds is its role in the creation of conflict. Each play portrays one or more couples in love and then shows their progress against various obstacles as they seek to be joined and to have their union accepted by those around them. In this, all plays share a common structure. The one constant is the lovers seeking accepted union; the variable is presented by the obstacles, concrete or abstract.

One essential difference between the two systems is the presence of rivals as obstacles in the pastorals. Stemming from the existence of an unmarried heroine, this situation results in momentary trouble for her and her lover as the rivals resort to ruse or even force to win her love. As such they represent concrete obstacles with which the hero and heroine must contend. The most serious obstacles to the love of the pastoral characters are much more abstract than the flesh and blood rivals, though nonetheless real. They result from social and family pressures arising from an acute consciousness of a rigid class society. Considerations of personal and family honor further strengthen this area of conflict, the true obstacle.

The proliferation of conflicts present in the pastorals contrasts

The Tragedies

with the simpler system of the tragedies. One difference is the structure of the social world of the tragedies, whose main characters represent a single social class. Pressures inherent in the stratified world of the pastorals cannot come into play in the tragedy. Whereas the pastoral characters find obstacles in their families, their social situation, and in the rivals, the barriers to love between the tragic hero and heroine have their origin in a political controversy. Refusal to obey orders from political authority, supposed betrayal of the homeland by loving a foreigner, outright rebellion or passive resistance—the hero's reaction to the politically initiated barrier to his love finally proves futile. The obstacle is as explicit as it is unassailable.

The only element in the pastorals which even approaches the strength and presence of political conflict in the tragedies is the role of the superhuman powers. The characters acknowledge the impossibility of escape from them, an inevitability equaling that of the political force in the tragedies. They see themselves helplessly trapped by superior forces opposed to their desire and accuse them of denying or actively attempting to destroy their love. Essential differences must be pointed out.

The gods never act directly against the pastoral hero and heroine. Another area of stress provides the true conflict. Furthermore, though they berate the superhuman powers, the pastoral characters display an ambivalent attitude, for they likewise expect help from heaven. In the final act of each of the three plays this latter attitude comes to the fore as a reversal or revelation takes place which is directly due to heaven's intervention. Everything works to the advantage of the good characters, while all incidents serve to denounce or destroy those who are evil. Though seemingly due to mere chance, these events are finally shown to be part of a providential plan to preserve hero and heroine. The characters who remain true to their beliefs by serving the cause of good are rewarded.

The tragic characters display the same belief in assistance from the gods in defense of innocence. The expected turn of events does not take place however. The strongest force at work proves in the end to be the political force. No greater power exists or makes known its existence in the context of the play.

The clearest example of this situation is provided by *Solyman,* the last tragedy. In this play nothing, no single incident, helps the position of the tragic lovers. Indeed every event—contrived or real—contributes to their downfall, eventually causing the death of nearly every character in the play. The total absence of such a providential side of happenings on earth is one of the most striking characteristics of the tragedies. Though the characters still call to the gods for help, expressing the belief that their prayers will be answered, there is no indication of the presence of superhuman powers to aid them. The characters recognize the futility of their situation upon realization of the gods' abandonment of the world.

In this respect the tragedy presents the exact opposite of the pastoral system. Although both are based on love and the conflicts which it creates, there exists a power in the pastorals which can easily sweep away any obstacles and join the couple in a happy ending. Family quarrels, social differences—all are forgotten as the strongest power in the play makes known its will. This power has, in effect, been held in abeyance until its intervention becomes absolutely necessary. The final outcome does not, however, appear as the work of a totally unexpected *deus ex machina.* Preparation for the intervention is evident through the characters' expressed belief and expectation of such a sign from heaven. In the most simple terms, they are innocent; heaven knows them to be innocent and must therefore protect them and prove their innocence.

Given a similar attitude in the characters of the tragedies and given also the fact that the plays end with their deaths, we may draw one of two conclusions. Either the hero and heroine are guilty, and their love truly represents a crime, or they are innocent, and there is simply no power greater than the political force which might save them. The latter must be accepted. Throughout Mairet's theater love is valued above all else. Only when it conflicts with the moral standard is it challenged, as seen in *Virginie.* In the other plays nothing is more sacred than love, from Chryséide's opening monologue about the sorrow of separation from her lover to Cleopatra's sincere defense of marital constancy. In short, nothing receives allegiance before love.

The constancy of the tragic characters results in their downfall, since it does not allow them to follow political orders. Such constancy triumphed in the pastoral world because of the presence of the superhuman powers. In the tragedies, especially *Solyman,* it is the lack of any such help which finally seals the doom of the lovers. The absence of any divine dimension stands as one of the most unusual features of Mairet's three tragedies. It is as though Mairet could conceive no tragedy in a world in which providence and the gods exist. Their absence alone defines the tragic atmosphere. The impossibility of help from superhuman powers creates the inevitability leading to the tragic outcome. Hope is present though unfounded. Love finally becomes the victim of the world situation in which there exists no power to save it.

CHAPTER 6

The Final Tragicomedies

BECAUSE of Corneille's success with *Le Cid* in 1636–37 authors generally abandoned production of tragedies. Reading the play's popularity as a sign of further change in audience tastes, the authors flocked to the genre in which most of them had begun their careers. They turned back to tragicomedy, and in the years 1637–39 plays of the irregular genre surpassed both tragedy and comedy.[1] In general the tragicomedy of the period reflected the atmosphere of classical tragedy rather than the highly animated spirit of the earlier tragicomedies. Dramatists observed the unities and took careful precautions not to shock the audience's proprieties.

Although they are tragicomedies, Mairet's four final plays do not conform to this pattern. As though completing his career in a circle, they revert to earlier models, ripe with action, and with elements of comedy bordering on farce. They violate both the unities and the proprieties. The plays, the ninth through the twelfth of his dramas, unfortunately show neither a deepening of his abilities nor even a continuation of established talent. One can only call them a futile attempt at regaining his earlier position of acknowledged greatness. The final tragicomedies represent a last gasp, as it were, after which Mairet totally, and without apparent regret, abandoned the theater. His last four plays are *l'Illustre Corsaire* (1637), *Roland Furieux* (1637–38), *Athénaïs* (1638–39), and *Sidonie* (1640). None procured for Mairet the desired critical or popular success.

I   L'Illustre Corsaire[2]

Mairet's first tragicomedy after the renunciation of tragedy, *l'Illustre Corsaire* presents a complicated story of pirates, a

The Final Tragicomedies

princess being unwillingly forced into marriage, the return of a lost prince, two foreigners disguised as madmen, and a gallant but unscrupulous king. Filled with disguise, deceit, some harmless and some not so innocent trickery, plus a happy ending, the play in some respects signals a return to the earlier world of the tragicomedy. It appears more specifically a cross between the comedy of the *Galanteries du duc d'Ossonne* and the tragicomic universe, including its pastoral elements. The play's emphasis falls decidedly on the side of comedy rather than on that of either measured tragicomedy or tragedy. The characters are Lepante, a Sicilian prince; Isménie, a princess with whom the hero is in love; Evandre, her doctor; Dorante, her brother; Armille, Félicie, and Célie, her lady and maids of honor; Lypas, king of Ligurie and also in love with Isménie; his confidant Erphore, and finally Tenare and Argant, two pirates.

Some ten years before the opening of the play Lepante and Isménie were two happy lovers about to be married. Heaven seemed to promise good tidings for them, and all would have proceeded accordingly for their marriage, except for Lepante's eagerness. Alone with Isménie in her chambers, he became too bold, and she angrily banished him from her sight. In despair Lepante threw himself from a window and landed in the sea below. No one ever found his body. Blaming herself for the death, Isménie eventually lost her mind. More than nine years passed before she regained her sanity and could return to her place in the court at Marseilles. By means of several lies purposely spread as rumors, the king, her father, explained both her absence and her return. At present she is to marry Lypas, a prince who has usurped her father's throne, although she still loves and mourns for Lepante. Evandre recounts all this to Lepante in the play's opening scene when the prince, having heard rumors of Isménie's death, returns to Marseilles. He asks the old doctor to devise a plan whereby he can see and speak to Isménie. Evandre says that he must "faire le fou" ("act like a foolish madman") and will thus be able to gain entrance to the court as a distraction to the princess's melancholy. Lepante decides to act the part of the sad fool, and Tenare, one of his lieutenants, will play the happy fool.

Evandre introduces his two fools to the court during the

second act. Tenare takes the stage first and amuses all gathered there with his antics, his poetry, and his new-born passion for Célie. *L'Illustre Corsaire* shows many aspects of a play within a play in this act. The actor-audience dichotomy on stage, the presentation of both improvised and previously rehearsed texts, one comic and one tragic character, even an intricate play between stage and true reality—these elements appear in several plays of the period. The judicious use of asides and comments by Célie and Félicie set Tenare's play at one remove from the true play, as though their remarks on his acting function as a verbal proscenium arch through which to perceive the reality of the game. Tenare himself later fulfills this function in relation to Lepante's story, as he drops hints and outright truths meant for the audience's ears only.

Lepante enters, having assumed the name "King Nicas," and tells his tale. He first saw Isménie as a vision in a dream, and he has come to serve as her slave. In response to her questions concerning his sadness, he relates the story of his unhappy love. It presents an almost perfect parallel to the reality of his situation of ten years ago. He concludes by saying that he has dwelt with Neptune ever since the unfortunate love affair broke off. Isménie does not fail to comprehend him and soon realizes that the mad king is her Lepante. In the third act he admits his disguise to her and tells of his life of the past ten years. A merchantman rescued him from the sea, but they were soon attacked by pirates who took Lepante prisoner. Hearing that Isménie had died, he vowed to remain with the pirates and seek his death. Isménie also tells a tale of pirates. A ship of Africans captured her brother but then released him under conditions not fully explained. He had nothing but praise for the courtesy and honesty of the pirate chief Axala. The rest of the court soon enters, and Lepante, as King Nicas, imperiously berates Lypas for daring to claim Isménie's hand. It should belong to him alone, as she would freely offer it if given the opportunity. In order to appease him, Dorante, the princess's brother, says that whomever she chooses will be her protector and husband. Without hesitation she chooses Nicas, and Lypas concedes defeat.

A serious barrier to the marriage arises, when in the fourth act Dorante makes known the conditions of his release by the

The Final Tragicomedies

pirates. He had to promise to surrender his sister to Axala if the pirate should demand her. The prince feels honor bound to respect the agreement to which he swore, and Axala has just had a letter delivered to Dorante in which he states that he will soon come to claim the princess. She pleads with Lepante to save her from such a wretched fate and promises to follow whatever advice he should give her. At first Lepante urges her to honor her brother's promise, since it was made in good faith. After another incredulous outburst by Isménie, Lepante reveals the truth. He is Axala, and for the past ten years he has been an honorable pirate. He recounts his story and ends by saying that his principal desire is to regain his throne. Rather than fight him in the open, the king and Erphore decide to feign acquiescence while plotting behind his back.

Their plan emerges at the beginning of the fifth act as the king kidnaps Isménie and Célie from their room. Two strangers, who later prove to be Lepante and Tenare, save them near the port, and defeat Lypas. At the same time subjects faithful to Lepante have taken up arms, and his flotilla has entered the harbor blocking all traffic. Lypas is deposed, and Isménie and Lepante can finally be married.

The recurring leitmotifs of disguise, trickery, and deceit tie the play to Mairet's comedy, the *Galanteries du duc d'Ossonne*. Of all the author's works *l'Illustre Corsaire* most resembles the comedy. Indeed, the word *galanterie* forms a theme of the play, as it indicates an action, not altogether trustworthy or honest, the goal of which is the accomplishment of love. As with the comedy, the tragicomedy's principal theme is change, and the characters direct all action toward the reestablishment of the original situation. In that, the two plays differ substantially, for as much as the *Galanteries* describes a constantly evolving state of affairs, *l'Illustre Corsaire* works through change and disguise in order to attain a previously existing equilibrium. The action is thus circular, but it presents a dramatic problem. The state which the characters hope to reach existed ten years before the play's opening scenes. From this situation arises the necessity of so many tales, stories, and lengthy expository remarks. The players in the present must also carefully delineate the past in order for the audience to understand the purpose of their frenetic activity. A similar problem existed in *Solyman,* resulting in the tragedy's hopelessly complicated plot line. Such a structure might seem more in keeping with tragicomedy than tragedy, but one may ask if the resulting confusion is really necessary in any genre.

L'Illustre Corsaire, however, does have the merit of following the unity of action, taken in a broad sense, as the play moves toward the union of Lepante and Isménie. Furthermore the action takes place off stage, thereby avoiding any undue social shock. Finally, the comedy borders on the farcical without becoming broad or scabrous. Indeed, the play's best moments arise in its comic scenes, and they renew the regret that Mairet did not exercise himself more in that genre.

II Roland Furieux[3]

Ariosto's *Orlando Furioso* proved a fertile field of inspiration for early seventeenth-century dramatists. La Calprenède based his tragicomedy *Bradamante* (1636) on it, as well as on Garnier's key tragicomedy. Du Ryer's *Alcionée,* a tragedy staged in 1637, dramatized an episode from canto 34 of the work. *Orlando Furioso* was reportedly the favorite literary work of the comte de Belin, Mairet's protector. That fact alone provides sufficient reason for the author's choice of Ariosto's romantic tale as the basis for his next play. Mairet's tragicomedy comes largely from cantos 18, 19, 23, 24, 28, 29, and 39.[4] He has made minor changes in Ariosto's story but in the main followed the plot line of the Italian work.

Hopelessly in love with Angélique, a beautiful pagan girl, and fearful that she has left him for another man, Roland has fled Paris and the court of Charlemagne in search of her. He opens the play with a long section of stanzas which properly express his inner turmoil. Although Roland realizes that his lord and the protection of the country demand his service, mere duty proves an insufficient reason in the face of love. The hero soon notices many names and verses carved on the surrounding trees. Upon seeing the names Médor and Angélique his fears seem well-grounded, but Roland justifies the use of the name "Médor" by explaining it as a discreet substitution

The Final Tragicomedies

for Roland. A peasant couple arrives, and Roland questions them about the identity of the two lovers. They reveal Médor to be Angélique's husband and show Roland a bracelet which Angélique gave them. The hero can no longer doubt the truth, and he wanders off into the woods. Médor and Angélique occupy the stage for the final scene of act I and the initial scene of act II. The heroine cannot believe that Roland would abandon Charlemagne. If it is true that jealousy has so overpowered the knight's reason, she fears for Médor's safety. He, of course, assures her of the valor she inspires in him.

While walking through the forest Isabelle comes upon Angélique, who is momentarily alone. The two girls marvel at each other's beauty and exchange stories. Isabelle, the daughter of the king of Galicia, is betrothed to Zerbin, son of the king of Scotland. At present he is searching for their horses, which have strayed. In this particular scene the author is most anxious to insist on the similarities between the two—they are equal in beauty, grace, and merit—and on an essential difference which stands between them—Isabelle is a devout and ardent Christian, whereas Angélique is a pagan. Soon, Zerbin arrives and announces that he has found Roland's horse.

The third act opens with further stanzas delivered by Roland. He complains that sorrow is destroying his powers of judgment and that "la jalousie infecte ma raison" ("jealousy has afflicted my reason"). He rages at the faithlessness of Angélique, and fury takes total control over him. He throws off his armor and demolishes trees and rocks. Zerbin and Isabelle find the sword and armor, and hang them on the tree in memory of Roland. They exit, and Rodomont, a pagan warrior, enters and finds Roland's sword. He decides to take it as his own, but Zerbin challenges him in response to the infidel's insolence. During the fierce battle Rodomont kills Zerbin.

Angélique begins act IV with a lyrical complaint expressed in stanzas speaking of Médor's tardiness. She still fears Roland's vengeance and the fury of his jealousy. When Médor finally arrives, he tells her of a group of peasants who begged him to save them from a raging monster. The beast is indeed Roland, who had earlier attacked them, killing several men.

According to Médor, they dissuaded him from more massacres only by throwing a freshly killed doe in his path, which he fell upon and devoured. Rodomont meanwhile has fallen in love with Isabelle, and he has made her promise to marry him. Unwilling to consummate such a marriage and anxious to remain faithful to Zerbin, she devises a plan by which Rodomont will kill her. She will preserve her honor and will not have committed the sin of suicide. In the fifth act Isabelle puts her plan to work. Rodomont, extremely drunk, agrees to grant Isabelle her liberty in exchange for a magic charm which will render him invulnerable to battle wounds. While actually praying to God for strength, she pretends to be incanting a mysterious magic formula. She explains to Rodomont that in order to prove its efficacy she has cast the spell on herself. He has only to stab her with his sword, and he will see its success. The pagan then strikes Isabelle killing her. In the play's final scenes Roland comes on stage pursuing several shepherds. After he has killed one, "le Sommeil sort de sa grotte" ("Sleep comes out of its cave") and overtakes the hero in a wrestling match. Astolphe arrives and cures Roland by pouring a magic potion in his ear. Upon awakening, Roland admits no recollection of his past deeds, only a nagging sense of having sullied his honor. Astolphe explains that all the troubles arose because Roland loved a pagan at the expense of France's salvation, the Christian faith, and his own duty. God has renewed his reason so that he can further combat his enemies and fight for the altars of the faith.

Although in some instances the various motifs do intertwine, *Roland Furieux* seems an uneasy juxtaposition of many disparate elements. In his eagerness to please the audience by presenting themes which had attracted attention elsewhere, Mairet sinned by including an overabundance of possible interests. The resulting work succeeds neither in eliciting a great deal of interest nor in creating a thematically unified whole. In this, of course, he errs by following Ariosto too closely. The play's main love interest, Médor and Angélique, functions in the idyllic register of the pastoral. The second couple, Zerbin and Isabelle, exist primarily as examples of Christian strength and virtue. Both men participate in the

The Final Tragicomedies

chivalric ethic of service to the lover and obedience to her wishes. The peasant couple, Bertrand and Bérénice, belong to a different world, that of commonsense peasants. With the shepherds they present elements which one can almost term farce, a far cry from the lyricopastoral tone of the young couples. Magic and interest in the supernatural play no small role in the play. Angélique possesses a ring which can make her invisible. Sleep manifests itself and visibly leaves its cave to aid Roland. Astolphe cures him with a magic potion, as he literally descends from heaven on his hippogriff—the very personification of a *deus ex machina*. Is the play a plea for Christian virtue; chivalric heroism; the pleasures of love; or defense of one's honor, country, king, or faith? The answer changes with each scene.

The most serious criticism of *Roland Furieux* is that it lacks the one unity essential to the creation of any play, that concerning the work's action. The tragicomedy has no real plot as it rambles from one scene to another. According to the play's ending, the religious element should stand paramount, and yet the audience clearly sympathizes with Angélique and Médor, the pagan lovers. Although Roland supposedly represents the hero, his awful acts, some of which take place on stage, repulse us as well as violate the proprieties. We can only share the relief of the peasants as Astolphe cures him, and he soars off to Paris on the hippogriff. The author, by creating confusion along the way, has failed to lead the audience to his moral ending.

Mairet realized that the episodic nature of *Orlando Furioso* prevented him from applying the unity of time to his theatrical adaptation. In the *advertissement* he stated that he had at least respected the unity of place.[5] Unfortunately the author, perhaps in his desire to please his patron, adhered much too closely to the original story's line of action. *Orlando* is almost cinematographic in technique, moving fluidly from scene to scene and from interest to interest. Any successful theatrical endeavor based on the work would of necessity have to concentrate on a relatively specific interest in order to create the sustained dramatic focus. Mairet's play is simply too disparate. In neither his personal invention nor his faithfulness to the Italian source did Mairet create the necessary focus to achieve a unified work. In the play's defense it must be said that several of the stanzas spoken by Roland and Angélique contain pleasing lyrical poetry. In this manner and also because of the use of machines (hippogriff, sleep descending, etc.) the tragicomedy looks forward to the seventeenth-century opera as well as looking backward to earlier dramatic forms.

III Athénaïs[6]

Mairet's eleventh play takes place in ancient Greece during the time of the emperor Théodose. Compared to the two preceding plays with their large numbers of characters, *Athénaïs* has a very restricted cast, numbering only seven. In addition to Théodose and his sister Pulchérie, members of the court include Tegnis, Pulchérie's confidante; Paulin, the emperor's confidant; and Phocas, captain of the guards. Athénaïs and Valère, a sister and brother of common blood, complete the list of characters.

Théodose opens the play, complaining to Paulin about the ungracious position loyalty must hold. He has no time for the joys of life or for the pleasures which Athens offers. The pomp costs him much but serves him little. When Paulin mentions marriage, the emperor grants that the good of the state dictates that he should marry, but he would rather not. Pulchérie enters and announces that a beautiful girl has come to present a plea. She asks Théodose to hide so that he can see the girl but not be seen by her. Phocas ushers Valère and Athénaïs into the throne room, and in turn each presents his side of the dispute. Their father died a short time earlier, and in his will he left all of his material possessions to the son, since he would have most need of them. To his beloved Athénaïs he bequeathed his knowledge, which, he felt, would bring her wealth and merit. Athénaïs agrees that she has received the greatest part of her father's fortune, but she asks her brother for enough money to live and pursue her studies. Furthermore, according to the unfortunate girl, a bitter sister-in-law has turned her brother against her. Pulchérie judges the will to be legal, granting all possessions to the brother, but she assures Athénaïs

The Final Tragicomedies

that she can depend on her friendship for future care. Having witnessed the scene Théodose has fallen in love with the beautiful girl. He describes his "agitation of mind and body" to Paulin and admits to being henceforth under a greater power than himself.

The second act begins three days later, during which time Athénaïs has been living at the court. She proclaims her admiration for the school of honor which Pulchérie has made of the court, but she admits to one embarrassment. She wants the esteem of the emperor but not his friendship, and she refuses to return his love. Tegnis calls her "the renown and glory of [her] sex" and admonishes her to accept what good fortune offers. As Théodose approaches, she flees to another room of the palace. Assuring Pulchérie that his love is "une flamme sans feinte" ("a true fire"), he asks her to help him.

The other characters express the fear that Théodose may harm himself or Athénaïs in his disturbed state, but Pulchérie refuses to believe that he would commit any act at the expense of his own glory and self-respect. They must find a way to make Athénaïs accept the marriage. Such was her original plan, Pulchérie admits. When Tegnis mentions the social difference between the two, Pulchérie responds that love makes all equal, and that a virtuous commoner on the throne would be no threat to her own position and power. Théodose and Athénaïs enter. After discovering that she alone stands against the marriage, the girl accepts. In an aside at the end of the act, Phocas says that something may yet present an obstacle to the marriage.

The obstacle proves to be religion. Not being Christian, Athénaïs refuses to marry Théodose. He prays that Heaven may send a miracle to convince the girl of her error. As the act continues, the emperor receives progress reports of the attempts to dissuade Athénaïs from her stance. But being extremely intelligent she can answer all the objections. Finally Paulin convinces her through his adroit reasoning. Athénaïs appears before Théodose and abjures her paganism. Heaven's goodness, the love of the emperor, and Paulin's mind all contributed to her conversion. The palm must go to Heaven, says Théodose, for creating love to light and rule the chaos of the world. Athénaïs asks that the wedding not take place for three days.

In the interval between the fourth and fifth acts something has happened to upset the emperor. The violence of his love has turned to anger, which he directs against Athénaïs. The confused girl cannot imagine what she could have done to deserve such treatment. Pulchérie finally discovers the truth of the incident. Théodose is angry at Athénaïs for having given away an apple which he had offered her and then claiming to have eaten it. Since she gave it to Paulin, Théodose believes her unfaithful. In truth, Pulchérie asked Athénaïs to give Paulin the apple because he was ill. The girl lied to the emperor for fear of angering him. She admits her error, he asks her pardon, and the two can finally be joined in marriage.

Besides violating the unity of time, which Mairet had respected in every play beginning with *Silvanire*, *Athénaïs* makes ruin of the unity of action. Except for remarks at the close of the acts, the play could just as easily end after act III or act IV as at the end of act V. All problems stand resolved at the conclusion of the two earlier acts. No one raises the religious issue until the fourth act, and though it is drawn from the life of the real Athénaïs, the apple incident in the context of the play seems a most obviously artificial addition to constitute a fifth act. A totally unnecessary sequence, it neither furthers the story nor aids in character development. The play possesses the weakest, most arbitrary construction of any of Mairet's works. The absence of any true conflict underlines this weakness. Because Pulchérie summarily dismisses any political or social arguments against the marriage, they play no role in the drama. The religious issue, of most interest historically, functions in the fourth act only.

In this act *Athénaïs* is a Christian conversion drama.[7] The means of conversion is simple argumentation. The members of the court attempt to point out to Athénaïs the errors of her pagan belief and in doing so to bring her to accept the Christian truth. They are careful that she be truly convinced of the religion's reality, that no force be used, and that she embrace Christianity of her own volition. It is stated as one of the fundamental laws of religion that freedom of election

The Final Tragicomedies

precede acceptance. In addition, she must not accept conversion merely in the hope of pleasing Théodose or for fear of displeasing him.

The conversion comes about as the result of a discussion between two equal parties, the one convincing the other of the justness of its reasoning. Heaven also must play a role in the process, and the characters admit that "un coup du Ciel" ("an act of heaven") would help matters. Showing faith in heaven's active role in the lives of men, as well as confidence in the final outcome, Pulchérie says: "Sa main, qui peut tirer la clarté des ténèbres, Gagne quand il luy plaît des combats plus célèbres" ("Its hand, which can separate light from darkness, is victorious when it wishes in more difficult battles") (IV. 3). The difficulty in the play is that the entire conversion scene—argumentation, reasoning, and final acceptance—takes place off stage, thereby nullifying any possible effect on the audience. A Christian Athénaïs appears before Théodose at the end of the act, but she does not seem a substantially different person. The reason for this is simply that in previous acts paganism played no role in her character. The audience has not come to know Athénaïs the pagan, but just Athénaïs, a character who does not change from one act to another. The movement of the character involves a change from a state of which the audience had no knowledge to another state which has virtually no dramatic use. The religious aspect does not even enter into the fifth act. It makes no difference in that act whether the heroine is pagan or Christian.

Had the religious obstacle played a role throughout the tragicomedy, rather than suddenly appearing in act IV, Mairet would have created an engaging, and possibly edifying, play. Before his death in 1637, Charles de Beaumanoir, bishop of Le Mans, belonged to the literary circle of Mairet's protector, the comte de Belin. His successor, Emeric Marc de la Ferté, had sheltered the author for several months in late 1637 after the death of Belin, and Mairet dedicated the play to him. It is likely either that the bishop suggested the conversion drama to him or that Mairet chose the topic specifically to please him. In the dedication he solemnly stated that the courts of Montmorency and Belin taught him "the ways of the world, propriety and Honor, but thanks to my good fortune I found in your house the consummation of that excellent nourishment so that I could pass from the study of earthly things to the knowledge of Heavenly affairs and the true wisdom found in the piety which you profess."[8] Unfortunately *Athénaïs* does not attest to inspiration from such wisdom. Because of the work's disjointed, episodic nature, Athénaïs's religious conversion functions on the same level as the apple story. Despite the possibilities inherent in the story, the play does not stand as a prime example of religious drama.

IV Sidonie[9]

Mairet's final dramatic work takes place in the court of Béréminthe, widowed queen of Armenia. Her son and daughter, Pharnace and Céphise; her advisor, Aristée; and the prime minister, Arcomeine, represent the court. Other characters include Sidonie, the minister's daughter; Cinaxare, a Lydian prince in love with her; his confidant Zopire; and Céphise's two maids of honor. Sidonie and Cinaxare, who has been fighting in service of Armenia, are to be married. In gratitude for his services, the queen has also granted him three provinces. Pharnace also claims to be in love with Sidonie, and he is angered that the council reached the decision for her to wed Cinaxare without his knowledge or consent. When he declares his love for her, she refuses to betray her promise to Cinaxare. Furthermore she is frightened both by his show of violence and by a dream in which a lion stole her from her lover's arms. Sidonie explains the dream to Cinaxare and promises not to marry anyone but him. Cinaxare learns the true reasons for the girl's fears from Zopire. His friend explains the other prince's ambition and anger.

The scene changes to the throne room, where the queen berates her son for his audacity and disrespect at questioning her decision. As though speaking to a spoiled child, she warns him that *moeurs,* not years, give a person authority and that he has not reached that stage. Pharnace vows to prevent the marriage, if only for his own pleasure. The queen can only hope that age will bring maturity to her son. The marriage must take place for her glory, she says.

The Final Tragicomedies

In the meantime, Pharnace has convinced Cinaxare of Sidonie's ambition to reach the throne by marrying him, and Cinaxare accuses her of being unfaithful. In confusion she flees, and, as Pharnace enters, Cinaxare turns his anger on him. Pharnace orders the other prince to stop the proposed marriage. The queen enters just as her son is about to draw his sword, and she rebukes him again for his insolence.

In the interval between the second and third acts, an oracle concerning Sidonie has come to light. She will make a king and a husband happy, and the scepter depends upon the marriage, according to the oracle. Cinaxare believes that Pharnace must now marry Sidonie, and together the two lovers mourn their fate. Pharnace also convinces the court of his claim to the girl. Since a conflict has arisen between the oracle and an earlier promise to Cinaxare, the high priest decides to draw a name from a jar. In that manner he will decide who shall marry Sidonie. Aristée draws Pharnace's name, and the court begins preparations for the wedding. Immediately numerous bad portents appear as warnings from the gods. Statues perspire, the dead king appears, and sacrificial blood splashes on the priest's face and robe. Even Pharnace fears the menacing signs.

In the fifth act Arcomeine reveals a truth which he has long hidden. Sidonie is not his daughter but a slave, and therefore all laws forbid her union with the prince. He found her as an infant, he says, showing the court a gold medal she wore. Aristée recognizes the medal and unveils the true identity of the heroine. Before he knew the present queen, the late king had been secretly married to the queen of Palmire. She died while giving birth to Sidonie. The nurse, carrying the child to her father, was attacked and the infant was lost forever. As they open the medal, a letter from the king falls out which explains the truth of the preceding story. In the end, the queen gives Sidonie to Cinaxare, since she cannot marry her half-brother, and the priest reinterprets the oracle to fit the circumstances.

Sidonie suffers from the same ills as Mairet's preceding tragicomedies. The plot moves clumsily from incident to incident with no true obstacle, adding twists which serve no other purpose than to help the story along. Such plot elements as the oracle, the supernatural signs, and the two explanations of Sidonie's origins in the last scene arrive with no preparation. An additional problem common to *Athénaïs* and *Sidonie* concerns the character portraits that Mairet has drawn. They do not have sufficient depth to become real characters and never succeed in gaining the audience's interest or sympathy. The final two plays are the author's weakest in this respect.

The lack of a well-defined conflict with the interest of hero and heroine presents the most immediate weakness of Mairet's last four plays. The conflicts found in the previous plays, such as social consciousness, the good of the state, and disagreement with political authority, all appear in the final tragicomedies, but they form a catalog of the author's previous forms of discord, rather than providing true dramatic conflict. In none of the plays does Mairet create a conflict at a basic enough level to pose a problem of major concern for the characters. In his earlier plays, one major and perhaps one or two minor conflicts placed characters in opposition to one another. Through their reaction to that opposition they moved toward the play's conclusion. Depending on the genre, the issue of prime concern reached its outcome to the benefit or detriment of hero and heroine. In the final tragicomedies, issues of conflict arise in one act to be resolved in the following act, with no remaining trace of the matter through the rest of the play. The works pass from one minor conflict to another with little unifying them into a single play, except that the cast of characters remains the same. The area of religious concern, Christianity versus paganism, creates the one realm of new dramatic interest in the final plays, although it occupies only the fourth act of *Athénaïs* and plays a minor though recurrent role in *Roland Furieux*.

Mairet's overdependence on trickery and supernatural happenings underlines the contrived nature of the plays. *L'Illustre Corsaire* depends almost exclusively on artifice for its dramatic conflict. In the course of the play, one can count almost a dozen situations and incidents, past and present, based on some means of disguising the truth. Supposed deaths, disguises and play-acting, truth presented as fiction, revelations of true identity—such are the play's sources of dramatic interest. The oracle in

The Final Tragicomedies

Sidonie, foreboding dreams and apparitions, a fated drawing, two disclosures of the heroine's identity, the gold locket and the late king's letter provide the impetus behind that play's plot, but they do not create a unified, viable work. For lack of a well-founded human conflict, the tragicomedies possess little of the dramatic life of Mairet's earlier works.

The principal weakness of Mairet's last five plays, *Solyman* and the tragicomedies, is the plot structure. The author either chooses a hopelessly confused plot, such as *Solyman* or *l'Illustre Corsaire,* or fails to project a single story line through five acts, as in *Athénaïs.* Apart from characterization, motivation, development, or any other dramatic feature, the plays fail because they either confuse or bore the audience. And because of the plots chosen by the author, they could hardly do otherwise. Mairet's skill was never truly in the construction of a story line. His best plays grew from already existing texts, judiciously selected by the author for dramatization. His acute dramatic sense, which early in his career led him to select feasible texts, apparently failed him later in his career. The chosen plot lines could not, without extensive revision, produce excellent plays. Dalibray's *Soliman* and Desfontaines' *Illustre Pirate* fare little better than Mairet's renditions of the same stories and fall into the same traps as do his plays. Mairet was once capable of exactly such reworking, as witnessed by his astute changes in the historical reality of Sophonisbe and Massinisse. Careful pruning of the plot of *Solyman* could have resulted in a moving, tragic play. Less dependence on the past of Lepante and Isménie could perhaps have made of *l'Illustre Corsaire* a swiftly paced active tragicomedy. Mairet did not see the weaknesses or the necessity of changes in structure. For that reason his later plays appear more amateurish and less carefully wrought than any of his earlier dramatic endeavors.

Apart from failing dramatic abilities, two other possible reasons arise for the obvious failure of Mairet's plays to live up to the promise of his earlier works. The first concerns Mairet's constant position as protected poet. Although it is difficult to say just to what extent the protectors played a role in the selection of his plots, Belin's literary pretensions, and those of the nobles and ecclesiastics around him, point to a plausible explanation for the choice of Mairet's final subjects. Rather than an inventive nature, Mairet possessed a mind which examined, criticized, and corrected existing material. To some extent his success depended on the choice of his source. Earlier in his career Mairet proved his ability to notice weaknesses in structure and actions which would sin against the proprieties or believability. He either did not note or chose to ignore the kinds of flaws rampant in his final sources. Eager to please his patrons, he possibly stilled his critical capacities and followed their directives.

In connection with Mairet's desire to suit his protectors' tastes, he most eagerly wanted to repeat his previous popular successes. Realizing that fame did not come from high-born affluent patrons alone, the author sought audience acclaim in his works. With the other authors, Mairet reverted to tragicomedy after 1637 and *Le Cid*. Judging the public reaction as expressing a desire for more plays like the early tragicomedies, Mairet tried to repeat former patterns. Because of the evolution in theatrical tastes, however, he misinterpreted the audience's wishes. While returning to tragicomedy, French theater of the seventeenth century did not instantly stop its forward progress. In the late 1630s Mairet erred by presenting plays which would perhaps have appealed to audiences of the late 1620s or early 1630s. His dramatic productions no longer coincided with the desires of the theatrical public. Theater's continuing evolution left him in its wake, as he searched unsuccessfully for past glory.

Conclusion

THE career of Jean Mairet, initiated in youthful promise, rose quickly to the heights of great success, but the author could scarcely enjoy his dominant position before he had to relinquish it, plunging with equal rapidity to oblivion. Passing from tragicomedy and pastoral to comedy, then tragedy, and finally back to tragicomedy, the path of his career traced a circle. His literary career, however, reached several important high spots before the descent into nothingness of his finally persistent lack of success. *Sylvie, Silvanire, Sophonisbe,* to a lesser extent the *Galanteries du duc d'Ossonne* and *Virginie,* mark the salient points of Mairet's dramatic art.

His role in the establishment of the classical unities and his success at proving the theory's efficacy in dramatic literature have always stood as his essential contributions to French theater. Behind these accomplishments lie several other achievements manifesting his talent, without which Mairet could never have realized the niche granted him by literary historians. The author created believable characters, endowing them with individuality and the means of expression proper to them. In his best works he placed them in situations which created true psychological dilemmas, as they faced conflict from those in power above them. This linking of character, expression, and action proved the key to the theory's success. Joining the disparate elements, Mairet helped in establishing French theater as truly dramatic.

Although the silence of his final forty-five years may attest to bitterness at his lost career, it is equally possible, especially with the calming effect of the passage of years, that Mairet gained the perspective to realize his importance. He had played an essential role in orienting theater toward its true identity, a valid literary expression of human joy, sorrow, and triumph, meaningful to contemporary spectators and to future audiences.

Notes and References

Chapter One

1. Jean Mairet, *L'auteur du vray Cid espagnol à son traducteur sur une lettre en vers qu'il a faict intitulée Excuse à Ariste* (Le Mans ?, 1637), in *La Querelle du Cid*, ed. Armand Gasté (1898; rpt. Geneva, 1970), pp. 67–69.
2. Pierre Corneille, *Advertissement au Besançonnois Mairet* (Paris, 1637), in Gasté, pp. 319–27.
3. Gustave Bizos, *Etude sur la vie et les oeuvres de Jean de Mairet* (Paris, 1877), p. 3.
4. Mairet, "Lettre de Monsieur Mairet à M. D. S.," in Gasté, pp. 333–41.
5. Quoted in Frères Parfaict, *Histoire du théâtre françois* (Amsterdam, 1735–49), IV, 339.
6. The act of baptism was discovered by H. Tivier and is reproduced in E. Dannheisser, *Studien zu Jean de Mairets Leben und Werken* (Ludwigschafen, 1888), p. 61.
7. Mairet, "Epistre dédicatoire" to *Les Galanteries du duc d'Ossonne*, ed. G. Dotoli (Paris: Nizet, 1972), p. 130.
8. Mairet, "Sonnet" from *Autres oeuvres lyriques du Sieur Mairet* published with *Silvanire* (Paris, 1631).
9. Mairet, "Ode" from *Autres oeuvres poétiques du Sieur Mairet* published with *Sylvie* (Paris, 1629).
10. Tallemant des Réaux, *Historiettes*, ed. Antoine Adam (Paris: Gallimard, 1960), I, 362–63. Tallemant mentions Théophile and Mairet in a footnote to this indication.
11. Mairet, "Ode à Monseigneur de Montmorency sur son Combat Naval, 1625" in *Autres oeuvres poétiques*.
12. Antoine Adam, *Théophile de Viau et la libre pensée française en 1620* (Paris: Droz, 1935), pp. 419–23.
13. Corneille, *Advertissement*, in Gasté, p. 321.
14. The text is reproduced in Marsan's edition of *Sylvie* (Paris: Droz, 1932), pp. xix–xxvi.
15. Fontenelle stated that it was "tant récité par nos pères et nos mères à la bavette." Quoted in Marsan, p. xii.
16. Mairet, "Epistre" in *Sylvie*, pp. 1–3.

17. Mairet, "Préface en forme de discours poétique, à Monsieur le Comte de Carmail" in *Silvanire* (Paris, 1631).
18. Mairet, "Epistre" in *Silvanire*, p. 3.
19. Mairet, "Epistre dédicatoire" in *Les Galanteries*, p. 130.
20. Mairet, "Epistre" in *Le Grand et dernier Solyman ou la Mort de Mustapha* (Paris, 1639).
21. La Pinelière, *Parnasse ou le critique des poètes*, quoted in Chardon, *Vie de Rotrou* (Paris: A. Picard, 1884), p. 80.
22. Tallemant, II, 774.
23. Tallemant, II, 774–75.
24. Segrais, *Segraisiana ou Mélanges d'histoire et de littérature* (Amsterdam, 1722), p. 144.
25. Mairet, "Epître dédicatoire" in *Sophonisbe*, ed. Dédéyan (Paris: Nizet, 1969), p. 6.
26. Corneille, *Advertissement* in Gasté, p. 326.
27. Corneille, *Advertissement* in Gasté, p. 323.
28. Mairet, "Epître dédicatoire" in *Marc Antoine* (Paris, 1637).
29. Mairet, "Epistre dédicatoire" in *Les Galanteries*, p. 133.
30. Mairet, "Epître dédicatoire" in *Marc Antoine*.
31. Chapelain, *Lettres de Chapelain*, ed. Tamizey de Larroque (Paris, 1880), I, 327–28.
32. Mairet, "Epître dédicatoire" in *Roland Furieux* (Paris, 1640).
33. Mairet, "Au Lecteur" in *Sidonie* (Paris, 1643).
34. Chapelain, *Lettres*, I, 186–87.
35. Mairet, "Epistre" in Théophile de Viau, *Nouvelles Oeuvres de feu M. Théophile*, ed. Mairet (Paris, 1641).

Chapter Two

1. S. Wilma Deierkauf-Holsboer, *Vie d'Alexandre Hardy, poète du Roi* (Paris: Nizet, 1947).
2. For general history of tragicomedy, see Marvin T. Herrick, *Tragicomedy: Its Origins and Development in Italy, France, and England*, Illinois Studies in Language and Literature, vol. 39 (Urbana: The University of Illinois Press, 1955). For additional information on this period of French tragicomedy, see H. Carrington Lancaster, *French tragicomedy, its origins and development from 1552 to 1628* (Baltimore: J. H. Furst, 1907).
3. Théophile de Viau, *Pyrame et Thisbé*, ed. J. Hankiss (Strasbourg, 1933).
4. Honorat Racan, *Arthénice ou les Bergeries*, ed. L. Arnould (Paris: Société des Textes Français Modernes, 1933).
5. For information on the early seventeenth-century audience, see

Notes and References

Maurice Descotes, *Le public de théâtre et son histoire* (Paris: PUF, 1964), chap. 2, "La Formation du Public," pp. 25–58.

6. Mairet mentions this phenomenon in his "Epistre dédicatoire" in *Les Galanteries*, p. 131.

7. See Jules Marsan, *La pastorale dramatique en France à la fin du XVIe et au commencement du XVIIe siècles* (Paris: Droz, 1933).

8. Although the first three volumes of d'Urfé's *L'Astrée* were published in 1607, 1610, and 1619, playwrights did not use the novel as source material until the mid and late 1620s.

9. Jean Rousset, *La Littérature de l'âge baroque en France* (Paris: José-Corti, 1954), chapters 1 and 2.

10. Mairet, *Chryséide et Arimand*, ed. H. C. Lancaster, Studies in Romance Literature and Language, vol. V (Baltimore: Johns Hopkins Press, 1925).

11. For dating of Mairet's plays, see Giovanni Dotoli, *La datazione del teatro di Jean Mairet* (Bari: Adriatica Editrice, 1970–71).

12. Speaking of this problem, Scherer says: "La fusion du théâtre des poètes et du théâtre d'action, qui ne sera réalisée qu'avec le classicisme, est la rêve inassouvi d'une époque de transition." "La littérature dramatique sous Henri IV et Louis XIII," in *Histoire des Littératures*, III, ed. Raymond Queneau (Paris: Gallimard, 1958), p. 275.

13. Lancaster, "Introduction" to *Chryséide et Arimand*, pp. 22–23.

14. Jacques Ehrmann, speaking of the pastoral hero in *Un paradis désespéré: l'amour et l'illusion dans l'Astrée* (New Haven: Yale University Press, 1963), p. 19, says: "La parole est le seul 'acte' auquel il ait droit."

15. Mairet, *Sylvie*, ed. Marsan.

16. For Lancaster, *A History of French Dramatic Literature in the Seventeenth Century* (1929–42, rpt. Gordian Press, 1966), part I, vol. I, p. 242, the play is "primarily a pastoral with a few elements of tragicomedy." Herrick, *Tragicomedy*, p. 150 sees the play as a skillful combination of the machinery of the pastoral with a chivalric romance. Finally, Adam, *Histoire de la littérature française au XVIIe siècle* (Paris, 1949), I, 206, calls the play "une sorte de comédie de moeurs."

17. See Marsan's introduction to his edition of the play.

18. See Marsan, *Pastorale dramatique*.

19. Descotes, *Public de théâtre*, chapter 3, "La *Sylvie* de Mairet; l'Education du public," pp. 59–90.

20. Jean Morel, *Jean Rotrou: le dramaturge de l'ambiguïté* (Paris: A. Colin, 1968), p. 88.

Chapter Three

1. See René Bray, *Formation de la doctrine classique* (Paris: Nizet, 1966), and H. C. Lancaster, "The Unities and the French Drama," *Modern Language Notes* XLIV (April, 1929), 207–17.
2. For Chapelain's own critical essays, see Chapelain, *Opuscules Critiques*, ed. Alfred C. Hunter (Paris: Droz, 1936) and Ch. Arnaud, *Les théories dramatiques au dix-septième siècle* (Paris, 1886).
3. François Ogier, "Préface au lecteur" in Jean de Schelandre, *Tyr et Sidon* (1628, rpt. *Ancien théâtre françois*), VIII, 18.
4. Ogier, "Préface," p. 13.
5. André Mareschal, "Préface" in *La Généreuse Allemande, deuxième journée* (Paris, 1631).
6. Chapelain, "Lettre sur la règle des vingt-quatre heures" in *Opuscules critiques*, pp. 113–26.
7. Chapelain, "Lettre," p. 123.
8. Chapelain, "Lettre," p. 113.
9. Mairet, "Préface" to *Silvanire*, ed. Richard Otto (Bamburg, 1890), pp. 9–22.
10. Mairet, "Préface" to *Silvanire*, p. 17.
11. Mairet, *Silvanire* (Paris, 1631).
12. Honoré d'Urfé, *Sylvanire* (Paris, 1625). For a detailed comparison of the two pastorals, see Marsan, *Pastorale dramatique*, pp. 375–82.
13. Mairet, "Préface" to *Silvanire*, p. 21.
14. Mairet, "Préface," p. 21.
15. Herrick, *Tragicomedy*, p. 150.
16. See Carol A. Pieroni, "Mairet: *La Virginie* and the French Classical Drama" Ph.D. diss. Fordham University, 1965.
17. Lancaster, *French Dramatic Literature*, part I, vol. II, pp. 520–27.
18. Mairet, *Virginie* (Paris, 1635).

Chapter Four

1. Mairet, *Les Galanteries du duc d'Ossonne*, ed. Giovanni Dotoli (Paris: Nizet, 1972). The text is also reproduced in E. Fournier, *Le théâtre français du XVIe et XVIIe Siècles* (Paris, 1871). Excerpts are found in André Tissier, *La Comédie au XVIIe siècle avant Molière*, Nouveaux Classiques Larousse (Paris: Larousse, s.d.), I, 20–47.
2. See Bizos, Adam, Fournier, and Victor Fournel, *Le théâtre au XVIIe siècle: La Comédie*, among others.
3. Jacques Scherer, "La littérature dramatique," pp. 288–89.

Notes and References

4. Tallemant des Réaux, *Historiettes*, I, 79–81.
5. André Stegmann, among others, mistakenly states this in *L'Héroïsme cornélien: genèse et signification* (Paris: A. Colin, 1968), II, 146.
6. Dotoli, p. 35.
7. Quoted by R. Lebègue, *Le théâtre comique en France de Pathelin à Mélite*, Connaissance des Lettres (Paris: Hatier, 1972), p. 176. Lancaster also notes this neglect in his *French Dramatic Literature*, part I, vol. II, pp. 567–70.
8. Dotoli, "Sources et tradition espagnole et italienne," in his edition, pp. 32–45.
9. See Jean Rousset, *L'Intérieur et l'Extérieur: essais sur la poésie et le théâtre au XVIIe siècle* (Paris: José Corti, 1968), pp. 127–40.

Chapter Five

1. For a discussion of baroque tragedy and the theme of vengeance, see Elliott Forsyth, *La Tragédie française de Jodelle à Corneille (1553–1640)* (Paris: Nizet, 1962), chapter 8.
2. Descotes, *Public de thèâtre*, chapter 2.
3. Adam, *Théophile de Viau*.
4. Forsyth, *Tragédie*, p. 324.
5. Segrais, *Segraisiana*, p. 144.
6. Lancaster states that he doubts this influence of Chapelain on Mairet, part I, vol. II, p. 696.
7. Mairet, *Sophonisbe*, ed. Charles Dédéyan (Paris: Nizet, 1969). The original edition of the play is from 1635.
8. Mairet, "Au Lecteur," p. 8.
9. A. Axelrad, *Le thème de Sophonisbe dans les principales tragédies de la littérature occidentale* (Lille: Bibliothèque Universitaire, 1956).
10. Corneille, "Au Lecteur" to *Sophonisbe*, *Théâtre Complet*, ed. Pierre Lièvre, Bibliothèque de la Pléiade (Paris: Gallimard, 1950), II, 771.
11. Mairet, "Au Lecteur," p. 9.
12. *Sophonisbe* IV, 2; *Chryséide et Arimand* II, 2; *Sylvie* IV, 1.
13. Lancaster, *French Dramatic Literature*, part II, vol. I, p. 29.
14. Jacques Scherer, *La Dramaturgie classique en France* (Paris: Nizet, s.d.), p. 117.
15. Mairet, *Marc Antoine* (Paris, 1637).
16. Jacques Guicharnaud, "Beware of Happiness: Mairet's *Sophonisbe*," *Yale French Studies* XXXVIII (1967), 205–20.
17. Mairet, *Le grand et dernier Solyman* (Paris, 1639).

18. Lancaster, *French Dramatic Literature*, part II, vol. I, pp. 36–39.
19. Mairet, "Dédicace" to *Solyman*.
20. Mairet, "Dédicace" to *Solyman*.
21. Mairet, "Au Lecteur" to *Solyman*.

Chapter Six

1. Lancaster, *French Dramatic Literature*, part II, vol. I, pp. 202–203.
2. Mairet, *L'Illustre Corsaire* (Paris, 1640).
3. Mairet, *Roland Furieux* (Paris, 1640).
4. Lancaster, part II, vol. I, p. 226.
5. Mairet, "Advertissement" to *Roland Furieux*.
6. Mairet, *Athénaïs* (Paris, 1642).
7. André Stegmann, *L'Héroïsme cornélien*, II, 75–77 speaks of the influence of Père Caussin and the Jesuits on the play.
8. Mairet, "Epître dédicatoire" to *Athénaïs*.
9. Mairet, *Sidonie* (Paris, 1643).

Selected Bibliography

This bibliography lists works by Mairet, and secondary sources in which he is the principal object of study or in which he receives prominent mention. General works on Corneille or the theater of the period often include references to the author, but those could not all be listed. Many will be found in the notes. Finally, there exist no English translations of any of Mairet's works.

PRIMARY SOURCES

1. Works by Mairet

Chryséide et Arimand. Paris, 1630.
Sylvie. Paris: Targa, 1628. With "Autres oeuvres poétiques," 1629.
Silvanire. Paris: Targa, 1631. With "Autres oeuvres lyriques."
Les Galanteries du duc d'Ossonne. Paris: P. Rocolet, 1636.
Virginie. Paris: P. Rocolet, 1635.
Sophonisbe. Paris: P. Rocolet, 1635.
Marc Antoine ou la Cléopâtre. Paris: Sommaville, 1637.
Le grand et dernier Solyman ou la mort de Mustapha. Paris: Courbé, 1639.
L'Illustre Corsaire. Paris: Courbé, 1640.
Roland Furieux. Paris: Courbé, 1640.
Athénaïs. Paris: Jonas de Brequigny, 1642.
Sidonie. Paris: Sommaville & Courbé, 1643.
GASTÉ, A. *La Querelle du Cid.* Paris: 1898. Reprinted by Slatkine in 1970. Includes texts of Mairet's pamphlets and letters written during the quarrel.
MANTERO, ROBERT. *Corneille critique et son temps.* Paris: Buchet/Chastel, 1966. Includes Mairet's "Préface" to *Silvanire* and Ogier's "Préface" to Schelandre's *Tyr et Sidon*, as well as Corneille's critical discourses.

2. Critical editions of Mairet's plays

Chryséide et Arimand. Ed. H. C. Lancaster. Studies in Romance Literature and Language, vol. V. Baltimore: Johns Hopkins Press,

1925. Contains excellent introductory material on Mairet's life, the play's sources, etc.
Sylvie. Ed. Jules Marsan. Paris: Société des textes français modernes, 1932. Includes text of "Comédie ou Dialogue de Philène et de Sylvie," believed by many to be of Théophile's authorship.
Silvanire. Ed. Richard Otto. Bamberg: 1890.
Les Galanteries du duc d'Ossonne, Vice-Roy de Naples. Ed. Giovanni Dotoli. Paris: Nizet, 1972. Over 100 pages of introductory essays on the play, sources, public reaction, and dramaturgy. The edition is marred by some twenty-five textual errors and the lack of a bibliography.
Sophonisbe. Ed. Charles Dédéyan. 2nd edition. Paris: Nizet, 1969. Includes general introduction and bibliography, plus Latin and Greek texts of Mairet's immediate sources.

3. Bibliography

DOTOLI, GIOVANNI. *Bibliographie critique de Jean Mairet.* Paris: Nizet, 1973. An exhaustive listing of works by Mairet and studies done of his plays, including iconography and theses.

SECONDARY SOURCES

AXELRAD, ALBERT H. *Le thème de Sophonisbe dans les principales tragédies de la littérature occidentale.* Lille: Bibliothèque Universitaire, 1956. Discusses sources for the Sophonisbe story, and Italian, English, and French versions, including Mairet's.
BIZOS, G. *Etude sur la vie et les oeuvres de Jean de Mairet.* Paris: 1877. A dated study, rendered even less valid by the author's acceptance of wrong dating for Mairet's plays.
CHADWICK, C. "The Role of Mairet's *Sophonisbe* in the Development of French Tragedy." *Modern Language Review* 50 (1955), 176–79. Argues against Dédéyan's view of the "crise sentimentale" in the play, seeing it at the end of the play and therefore less important.
DANNHEISSER, E. *Studien zu J. de Mairets Leben und Werke.* Ludwigshafen am Rheim: J. Waldkirche, 1888. An excellent and lengthy study, especially good for Mairet's life.
———. "Zur Chronologie der Dramen des J. de Mairet." *Romanische forschungen* 5 (1890), 37–62. Corrects long-standing erroneous dating of Mairet's works.
DAWSON, F. K. "The Notion of Necessity in Mairet's *Sophonisbe.*" *Nottingham French Studies* 7 (1968), 57–66. Discusses the play

as exemplary of the early seventeenth-century tragedy, where the characters' decisions based on reason function as necessity leading to the play's conclusion.

DESCOTES, MAURICE. *Le public de théâtre et son histoire.* Paris: Presses Universitaires Françaises, 1964. Includes a chapter on public reaction to *Sylvie* as representative of essential changes in the seventeenth-century theatrical audience.

DOTOLI, GIOVANNI. *La Datazione del teatro di Jean Mairet.* Bari: Adriatica Editrice, 1970–71. Summation of all known information on the problem of dating Mairet's plays.

GUICHARNAUD, JACQUES. "The Impossibility of Happiness: Mairet's *Sophonisbe.*" *Yale French Studies* 38 (1967), 205–21. The author analyzes the play as the quest for happiness which the cruelty of the universe forbids.

KAY, WILLIAM B. "The Theatre of Jean Mairet: The Metamorphosis of Sensuality." Ph.D. dissertation, UCLA, 1965. An examination of the plays in terms of the moral and aesthetic values within them, viewing sensuality as the dominant theme.

KOHLER, P. "Sur la *Sophonisbe* de Mairet et les débuts de la tragédie classique." *Revue d'histoire littéraire de la France* XLVI (1939), 56–70. A study of Mairet's role in the development of classical theater.

LA CHARITÉ, RAYMOND C. and VIRGINIA. "Mairet's *Sophonisbe*: Character and Symbol." *Neophilologus* 54 (1970), 131–37. A study of the heroine as "the idealized image of the triumph of the self," whose predominant value is liberty, which she ultimately finds in choosing her death.

LANCASTER, H. CARRINGTON. "The Introduction of the Unities into French Drama in the 17th century." *Modern Language Notes* 44, no. 4 (April, 1929), 207–17. Discusses the role of Mairet and his *Silvanire*.

―――. "Leading French tragedies before the *Cid.*" *Modern Philology* 22 (1924–25), 375–78. Briefly mentions Mairet's *Sophonisbe,* among others.

―――. "Scarron and Mairet." *Modern Language Notes* 67 (1952), 470. Mentions quote in Scarron's *Jodelet ou le maître valet* (II. 3) of verses from Mairet's *Virginie* (IV. 3).

MARSAN, JULES. *La pastorale dramatique en France à la fin du XVIe et au commencement du XVIIe siècles.* Paris: Hachette, 1905. Importance for Mairet is chapter 9, "La Pastorale et les origines du théâtre classique." Shows the author's debt and contribution to the genre.

PIERONI, CAROL A. "Mairet: *La Virginie* and French Classical Drama." Ph.D. dissertation, Fordham University, 1965. An edition of the play with notes and introduction.

SCHERER, JACQUES. "La littérature dramatique sous Henri IV et Louis XIII," in *Histoire des Littératures*, vol. 3, pp. 273–98. Ed. Roger Caillois. Paris: Editions de la Pléiade, 1958. Discusses Mairet's role in the creation of French classical theater. Excellent introduction to the period.

SIMON, ROLAND HENRI. "A propos de 'Classicisme': la *Sophonisbe* de Mairet." *Kentucky Language Quarterly* XIX (1972), 65–81. A general study of the structure, dramaturgy, and characterization of the play, emphasizing the elements which make of it a classical tragedy.

TIVIER, H. "Relations de la France et de la Franche-Comté pendant la Fronde. Négociations de J. de Mairet." *Revue historique* XXV (1884), 43–68. Essential information on Mairet's life and his short-lived career as a diplomatic agent.

WADE, G. E. "Mairet's *Galanteries du duc d'Ossonne*. Two incidents." *Romance Notes* 6, no. 1 (Autumn, 1964), 57–59. Gives as possible sources for two striking incidents in Mairet's comedy Alarcón's *La Verdad sospechosa* and Tirso's *Vergonzoso en palacio*.

Index

Adam, Antoine, 15
Aiguillon, Duchesse d', 23
Angennes, Julie d', 21
Anne d'Autriche, 24
Appien of Alexandria, 104
Ariosto: *Orlando Furioso*, 24, 29, 136, 139

Balzac, Guez de, 13
Beaumanoir, Charles de, 143
Belin, François d'Averton, comte de, 19-20, 22-24, 87, 143
Bellerose, 16
Benserade, Isaac: *Cléopâtre*, 21
Boisrobert, François le Metel, Abbé de, 22, 25; *Pyrandre et Lisimène*, 72
Bonarelli, Prospero: *Solimano*, 120
Brun, Antoine, 13

Cardouan, Jeanne de (wife), 26
Carmail, Adrien de Montluc, comte de, 17-18, 61
Castro, Guillén de, 11
Chapelain, Jean, 20, 23, 25, 57, 59-61, 62, 63, 101; "Lettre sur la règle des vingt-quatre heures," 59-60
Corneille, Pierre, 11, 12, 21, 22, 27, 87; "Advertissement au Besançonnois Mairet," 11, 15; *Le Cid*, 21-22, 29, 106, 148; *Clitandre*, 72; "Excuse à Ariste," 11; *Mélite*, 87; *Sophonisbe*, 104; *Le Veuve*, 22
Clerget, Marie (mother), 12
Colletet, Guillaume, 13
Condé, Henri II, Prince de, 25-26

Dalibray, Charles Vion: *Soliman*, 21, 121

Desfontaines: *Illustre Pirate*, 147
Du Ryer, Pierre, 29, 87; *Alcionée*, 136

Fauche, Catherine (grandmother), 12
Ferté, Emeric Marc de la, 24, 43
Fiesque, comte de, 21, 101

Garnier, Robert, 97, 136; *Bradamante*, 29; *Hippolyte*, 97; *Les Juifves*, 97
Gaston d'Orléans, 18
Godeau, Antoine, 59-60
Grevin: *Caesar*, 97
Guarini: *Pastor fido*, 31

Hardy, Alexandre, 28-32, 34, 59, 98-99; *Coriolan*, 112
Hautefort, Marie de, 24
Henri IV, 14, 84
Hôtel de Bourgogne, 16, 20-22, 87-88, 98, 101, 120; see also Chronology

La Calprenède: *Bradamante*, 136
La Pinelière, Guérin de: *Parnasse*, 19
La Taille, Jean de: *Saül*, 97
La Valette, Louis de Nogaret d'Epernon, cardinal de, 17-18, 61
Le Noir, Mademoiselle (actress), 19-20
Livy, 104
Louis XIII, 18, 19, 25

Mairet, Gabriel (great-grandfather), 11
Mairet, Jean (grandfather), 12
Mairet, Jean (father), 12

161

Mairet, Jean: family background, 11; early life, 12-13; protection of Montmorency, 14-19; protection of Belin, 19-23; involvement in quarrel of the *Cid*, 21-22; connection with Richelieu, 25; diplomatic career, 26-27

WORKS:

Athénaïs, 24, 130, *140-44*, 147
Chryséide et Arimand, 15, 16, *34-45*, 64, 68, 80, 87, 107
"Comédie ou dialogue de Philène et de Sylvie," 16, 46
Galanteries du duc d'Ossonne, Les, 20, 23, 63, *84-96*, 133, 135, 149
Grand et dernier Solyman, Le, 18, 21, *120-27*, 130-31, 147
Illustre Corsaire, L', 22, *130-36*, 146-48
Marc Antoine, 21, 23, *113-20*, 125
"Préface en forme de discours poétique," 61-62
Roland Furieux, 22, 24, 130, *136-40*, 146
Sidonie, 24, 130, *144-46*
Silvanire, 17, 18, *61-72*, 95, 100, 116, 142
Sophonisbe, 20, 21, 22, 24, 77, *100-113*, 115-20, 126, 127, 149
Sylvie, 15-17, 18,, *45-56*, 64, 68-69, 77, 79, 87, 93-94, 100, 107, 149
Virginie, 20, *72-83*, 106, 130, 149
Mareschal, André, 29, 59; preface to *La Généreuse Allemande, deuxième journée*, 59
Mazarin, Cardinal, 26-27
Mellin de Saint-Gelais, 104
Molière, Jean Baptiste Poquelin, 88
Monroy y Silva, Cristobál: *Las Mocedades del duque de Osuna*, 84-85
Montchrestien: *L'Escossaise*, 97; *Sophonisbe*, 104
Montdory, 19-20
Montemayor: *La Diana*, 31

Montmorency, Henri II, duc de, 13-19, 23, 126, 143
Montmorency, Marie Félicie des Ursins, duchesse de, 18, 126-27
Montreux, Nicolas de (Olénix du Mont-Sacré), 104

Ogier, François, 29, 60; preface to Schelandre's *Tyr et Sidon*, 58-59
Osuna, Don Pedro Girón, Duke of, 84

Pichou, 29
Philip IV, king of Spain, 84
Plutarch, 99

Quarrel of the *Cid*, 11, 21-22, 95

Racan, Honorat: *Arthénice ou les Bergeries*, 30, 32, 39, 48, 56
Rambouillet, Catherine de Vivonne, marquise de, 20
Richelieu, Cardinal, 17, 22, 23, 25, 127
Rotrou, Jean, 19, 22, 87, 101; *Hercule Mourant*, 101, 112

Scarron, Paul, 19; *Le Roman Comique*, 19
Schelandre, Jean de: *Tyr et Sidon*, 29, 58
Scherer, Jacques, 87
Scudéry, Georges de, 11, 12, 19, 21
Segrais: *Segraisiana*, 20, 101
Seneca, 97, 101

Tallemant des Réaux: *Historiettes*, 14, 19-20, 84
Tasso: *Aminta*, 31, 34
Théâtre du Marais, 19-20, 121; *see also* Chronology
Théophile de Viau, 13, 15-17, 26, 56; "La Maison de Sylvie," 17; "Nouvelles Oeuvres, 15, 26; *Pyrame et Thisbé*, 15, 30, 38, 39, 48, 99-100, 112
Trissino: *Sofonisba*, 104

Index 163

Urfé, Honore d': *L'Astrée*, 30-32, 34-38, 39, 40, 41, 64; *Sylvanire*, 64, 67-68, 70-71

Valleran-le-Comte, 98

Viau, Théophile de. *See* Théophile

Villeroy, Maréchal de, 26

Vieux Comédiens du Roi, 98-99

Villiers, Claude Deschamps, sieur de, 98

Voltaire, François Marie Arouet de, 104